SEE YOURSELF

— *with* —

Friendly Eyes

SEE YOURSELF

— *with* —

Friendly Eyes

How to Let Go of Guilt

ILSE SAND

Translated by Mark Kline

First published by Gyldendal, Denmark in 2020
English language edition first published in 2023

www.ilsesand.com
Copyright © Ilse Sand 2023

Translation Copyright © Mark Kline.

ISBN 978-87-92683-26-7

eISBN 978-87-92683-27-4

Cover: Cinque

Photo of the author: Anne Kring

Illustrations: Kirstine Sand

Translated into English by Mark Kline

CONTENTS

FOREWORD

Figuratively speaking, you can say that the conscience is where you evaluate yourself. You're probably reading this book because you occasionally judge yourself harshly.

Self-evaluation can be realistic, but often it's influenced by many factors that can make it much too negative.

It's good to be able to feel guilt and have a bad conscience. It shows that you're a responsible person who cares about contributing positively to your own life as well as the lives of others.

You're probably not conscientious in every aspect of life. Some people are serious about being environmentally responsible, while others take on a lot of responsibility for solving practical problems. This book is primarily about the responsibility we take in relationships.

Some people are quick to take responsibility for bad vibes, for example, for someone not doing well or feeling hurt, and burden themselves with exaggerated guilt.

Others rarely or never see themselves as being guilty of anything negative.

Most of us are somewhere in between these two poles. But we can swing a bit back and forth in our lives. We can have good days or long periods of time where we see ourselves and our lives in a positive light. Then bad days come along when we overburden ourselves with criticism and bad conscience and feel we don't measure up.

When I was a pastor, I listened for many years to people weighed down with guilt or a bad conscience. Since then, as a psychotherapist, I've had the opportunity to help people examine their emotions on a deeper psychological level.

In addition, I've experienced how much more energetic I felt after realising that some of my guilty conscience was unrealistic or exaggerated. More about that in the introduction.

In this book, you'll find a number of tools for cleaning up your bad conscience and training to see yourself with a friendly eye. Among other things, it describes how you can make changes in the principles and rules you've formed in your life, get rid of the guilt that belongs to others, make friends with your fear, let go of struggles that exhaust you, and find strength in acknowledging the guilt that is yours, sharing it with others if relevant — and forgiving yourself.

The first chapter of the book explains what a bad conscience is, and it also explains how self-criticism can sometimes be used positively, while at other times, it's just a bad habit.

Three chapters are about a lack of responsibility. It's likely that one or more of your closest friends or family members shun the blame when something bad happens. If you easily develop a bad conscience, you're a prime target for people who want to unload their guilt and responsibility. That's why it's important to be aware of the mechanisms involved and how to protect yourself.

At the end of each chapter, you will find exercises to help you understand your feelings of guilt or inadequacy so you can better distinguish between which of the feelings are rational and which are out of proportion.

In the back is an overview of the book's tools and a test to measure your tendency to form a guilty conscience.

Instead of "he" or "she," I've chosen to use "she" throughout the book when referring to people of unknown gender.

I wish you the very best in your journey of discovery in your conscience, your relationships, and yourself.

- Ilse Sand, Hald Hovedgaard

INTRODUCTION

Valdemar feels guilty if he doesn't answer his phone when his mother calls. So he always answers — even when he doesn't want to be disturbed. Tue loves bananas and wants to empty the fruit bowl at his work, but he gets a bad conscience if he eats more than one. Rikke hates to exercise, yet she goes out on a short run a few times a week; otherwise, she'll feel guilty for not keeping her vow to stay in good shape.

Guilt, self-recrimination, and a bad conscience all play a part in governing our behaviour. We don't just do exactly what we want to; we show consideration, make room for others, share our things, and try to stick to the deals we make with ourselves.

I've always tended to develop a guilty conscience easily, even when I was a little girl on a farm in Vendsyssel, Denmark. Once, I caught two toads and fixed up a tub with sand and water for them to swim in. Then I forgot all about them. Later on, when I finally remembered and went down into the basement to check on the toads, they were dead. I wasn't very old, but I understood it was my fault they died. It made me unhappy, and I felt too ashamed to tell anyone.

Even though I still tend to take on too much responsibility, I also know something about showing a lack of responsibility.

When it comes to practical, everyday chores, sometimes I manage to make myself invisible until someone else steps up to do them.

It's different with the pain my loved ones endure. One day I visited my mother at the Aalborg Hospital. While passing through one of the wards, I walked by a mirror and smiled at myself. I was proud of how I had managed to slip this visit into my busy life and drive all the way from Djursland, a peninsula in Jutland, to Aalborg, one hundred thirty kilometres further north, even though driving exhausts me.

Two hours later, my image in that same mirror confronted me, and I shrank back in fright. My face was yellow and ashen, and I looked like someone with serious depression. I was overwhelmed by a guilty conscience, which prevented me from thinking clearly.

Back then, I wasn't sure what had drained me most from being with my mother. Possibly her story about the woman in the bed next to hers, whose son visited her every day, even though he lived a lot farther from the hospital than I did. Or the expression in her eyes when she looked at me. Or it might simply have been the tenuous emotional connection between us.

In periods of my childhood as well as my adult life, the predominant emotion I felt in relation to my mother was guilt. I knew it was irrational, yet it took me decades to escape its clutches and give room to the emotions hidden behind it.

Among other things, what helped loosen its grip was an insight into the mechanisms involved in guilt and responsibility, which made me aware of the limits of my responsibility. And when I realised that a bad conscience could cover up other emotions, it all made sense to me. My freedom came when I was able to accommodate the helplessness and sorrow that trickled out when my guilt began to dissolve. Recovering my right to be a completely average person with completely normal feelings such as anger, helplessness, and joy felt truly liberating.

I hope my experiences from my work as a pastor and psychotherapist, as well as from my personal life, can help you let go of any exaggerated feelings of guilt you may have, so you can see yourself with friendly eyes, feel more whole, and be more comfortable in your relationships.

CHAPTER 1

Guilt and Bad Conscience

A bad conscience arises when you do something that has negative consequences. Maybe your friend was looking forward to getting together with you, and you cancelled. Or maybe you'd vowed to go to the training centre, and instead, you stretched out on the couch.

To be guilty = to be the cause of something bad

A bad conscience is the distressing feeling of having done something that hurts yourself or others or that contradicts your own or others' values. Or of having neglected to do something you or others feel you should have done. As you can see, feelings of guilt and bad conscience are basically the same things, and I use the two terms interchangeably throughout the book.

A bad conscience can lead you *and* mislead you. Sometimes it motivates you to make up for something. Other times it might pressure you into doing more than you feel you can or into compromising with yourself and your values.

The strength of your guilty feelings says more about you as a person than it does about your guilt. You can be at fault without feeling guilty. And you can feel guilty without actually being at fault.

Likewise, sometimes your bad conscience says more about the person your guilt is focused on or your relationship with that person than it says about you. If you take the test in the back of this book, you'll discover that thinking about different people while taking the test affects the results. You've probably noticed how you can feel guilty about some small misstep — arriving five minutes too late, for example — when it involves a certain person, while it doesn't bother you in the least with someone else.

There can also be a difference in how serious your bad conscience is when it's aimed at yourself instead of someone else.

———————

An example:

Even though I do something like promise myself to relax all day Saturday and make no plans, it can happen that I can't say no to a friend who wants to hang out with me. If I said no to him, he'd feel bad, and that would make me feel guilty.

— Karina, age 28

———————

Karina chooses what makes her feel least guilty — saying yes to her friend's invitation. Someone else might have had no problem saying no to the friend because that person takes the promises she makes to herself very seriously, and she would feel guiltier breaking her vow than saying no.

Rational or irrational

If your bad conscience is more or less appropriate to what you have or haven't done, it's rational guilt. If you're standing in line and you push someone, and your bad conscience motivates you to apologise, that's fine. If you feel guilty about eating an ice cream sundae while you're on a diet to lose weight — or don't exercise as you planned, or in some way don't live up to your resolutions or values — your bad conscience can push you in the right direction.

If you feel guilty without knowing precisely why or because of an accident or situation out of your control, your bad conscience is irrational.

Rational bad conscience: The strength of your guilty feelings corresponds to the degree of influence you had on the situation and to the extent of the damage it caused.

Irrational bad conscience: Your feelings of guilt are overblown in relation to the situation.

It's important to be able to distinguish between these two types of bad conscience. They have to be handled in different ways. You need to recognise irrational guilt as inappropriate or as the misinterpretation of the reality it often is. You can read about how to work on an irrational bad conscience in Chapter 11. Here we will focus on the rational form.

Feelings of guilt appropriate to your pertinent situation must be faced up to, but they should not be allowed too much control of your choices in life.

If it's difficult for you to acknowledge your rational guilt and sense your bad conscience, you can easily fall into using inappropriate strategies that end badly for your relationships with others.

Typical attempt to avoid a bad conscience

If it was possible to always make everyone happy, including yourself, you could avoid a bad conscience. Unfortunately, that's seldom the case. Often you have to make choices and prioritise. If you're invited to two parties happening on the same day, you're going to disappoint someone. If you choose to spend your weekend working in your yard, you might feel guilty about not cleaning your house and, therefore, not living up to your standards of cleanliness — or about not visiting a friend who really needs to see you.

The question is how you handle your bad conscience. The two most commonly used strategies are explained below. I call the first one the ostrich method, which refers to the animal sticking its head in the sand to avoid seeing something that frightens it. I've named the second one the ant strategy because, besides being small, ants are very hard-working.

The ostrich method — some people won't acknowledge that they have made choices. They can always explain why they had to do what they did or that they did it because of someone else.

The ant strategy — other people do everything possible to make everyone around them happy and satisfied in hopes of not causing anything bad to happen. If, in spite of their efforts, they fail and people become disappointed, they compensate in every way they can, for example, by being extremely cooperative, pleasing, or self-effacing.

Both of these strategies make relationships difficult. If you use the ostrich method, it's difficult for you to reconcile after a conflict. It's not easy to meet halfway and help each other bear the responsibility for, let's say, a bad atmosphere between you if you don't think you're at all to blame for what caused it.

If you use the ant strategy, you probably get exhausted easily and begin to care less and less for the other person whose expectations or demands you don't put limits on. Besides that, you're running a high risk of becoming stressed out or developing depression. And you make yourself small by becoming the slave of other people's expectations.

In the following chapters, I will introduce alternative strategies to use if you're weighed down by guilt. First, let's examine the emotions involved in bad conscience.

The ingredients of a bad conscience

We can distinguish between *basic emotions* and *complex emotions*. Basic emotions are seen in people in all cultures and nations and in higher-developed species of the animal kingdom. All other emotions can be explained as various hybrids of basic emotions.

There is no agreement on which emotions should be considered the basic emotions. But all psychologists do agree that the following four belong in that category:

- Anger
- Fear/Anxiety
- Sadness
- Happiness

These four are enough to explain most of the emotions we feel. Disappointment, for instance, is a mixture of sadness and anger, while excitement is a mixture of anxiety and happiness.

All four basic emotions can be involved in a guilty conscience. Anger typically turns inward.

- **Anger:** You reproach or blame yourself.
- **Fear:** You fear the anger or judgment of others or yourself. Or you're afraid that, in some way, things are going to go badly for you.
- **Sadness:** You wish that you or others had acted differently or that the situation was different.
- **Happiness:** You are grateful or maliciously happy because an accident happens to someone else and not you.

Here are a few examples of a guilty conscience that contains three or four of the basic emotions:

One day, when I was stressed out, I didn't see a car, and I hit it and dented it. Later on, I felt guilty. I blamed myself for not being alert enough in traffic. Was scared that my boyfriend and the other driver were angry. Sorry about the money the dent would cost me and also because I had to admit to myself that I'm not quite the perfect driver I thought I was. But I am a little bit happy that my car only got a small scratch, not a dent like the other car.

— Jane, age 25

I'd been playing games on my computer all day, even though I'd promised myself to pick up around the apartment. I had a guilty conscience that evening. I was angry at myself because I hadn't gotten it done. Afraid that everyone would criticise me because my apartment was messy and dirty. Felt bad because it looked that way — and because I apparently can't live up to this image I have of myself of being neat and disciplined.

— Ulla, age 38

It's seldom that being sad causes problems. It's a healthy reaction that makes others — as well as yourself — want to help or take care of you. On the other hand, anger turned inward can exhaust you. And the fear of your own or others' anger or criticism can lead to self-repression.

You can read more about this in the following chapters.

Exercise:

Think of a situation where you have a guilty conscience. Consider to what degrees the various basic emotions are involved. If you wish, put a percentage on every emotion.

For example:

Anger turned inward: 20%.
Fear: 70%
Sadness: 8%
Happiness: 2%

Summary of Chapter 1: Guilt and bad conscience

A bad conscience consists of basic emotions: anger, fear, sadness, and perhaps once in a while, a bit of happiness, too. Guilt can be either rational or irrational, the latter being out of proportion to the situation.

Some people always deny they are to blame for any negative situation, while others struggle hard to be perfect in hopes of avoiding a guilty conscience. Fortunately, there are other options. We'll look closer at this in the following chapters.

CHAPTER 2

Discover the message in the anger you turn inward

Anger turned inward — typically in the form of self-criticism or self-recrimination — can lead to headaches, depression, and much else that is harmful. But it can also have a positive function. Let's begin with that before we turn to the negative consequences.

Sometimes scolding yourself can stop others from doing the same to you. If you've made a mistake that harms others and you appear to feel guilty about it, they will be less angry at you than if you take it lightly and pretend nothing happened.

Turning anger inward can also motivate you to do something good for yourself. If you buy an ice cream sundae while trying to lose weight, your self-recrimination may force you to stick the dessert into the freezer instead of ruining your diet.

Self-criticism can also help initiate change from a broader perspective.

An example:

Whenever I've felt bad over a longer period of time, an inner voice starts screaming: "Come on, you need to change something here. What you're doing isn't working!" Sometimes the voice can shove me out of my comfort zone and get me to do something I normally wouldn't dare do, like taking a trip by myself or calling a professional for help.

— Uffe, age 48

Self-criticism can motivate you to change a way of living that's no longer in your best interests. It can also lead you to do good things for others.

If you've forgotten your mother's birthday, for example, your anger might tell you, "You can do better than this." And maybe your anger is right. You can choose to listen to it and do what it wants you to — for example, to make up for something.

Allow yourself to be corrected by self-criticism

When we realise that something bad is our fault, sometimes it's relatively easy to remedy the situation by apologising and perhaps trying to make up for it. If you've forgotten your mother's birthday, you can offer to stop by another day or send a bouquet of flowers. If you're genuinely sorry about what you have or haven't done, merely expressing your regret can be enough for you or the other person to be satisfied and forget about it.

There's no expiration date for apologies. It's never too late.

If once in a while you don't act on a rational guilty feeling, possibly it's somewhere inside, gnawing at you more than you think.

____

An example:

Once, I had a good friend for many years. I was so happy to have her. But one day, we decided to stop seeing each other because a conflict we couldn't resolve ruined how we felt about each other. Ida wrote me a very sweet farewell email, going out of her way to thank me for all the good times we had together. Back then, I was so angry that I didn't answer. But over the years, I've thought now and then about how it was actually a very sweet, very loving email, and I feel guilty about deleting it.

— Hanne, age 55

____

It would be relatively easy for Hanne to take care of this problem. And it probably would give her a greater sense of self-satisfaction than she thinks. For example, she could write:

Dear Ida

It's been a long time now, but I'm sure you remember me. When we broke off our friendship in 2004, you wrote me a very sweet and affectionate email to say goodbye. It took me many years to be able to appreciate that. It was very thoughtful of you, Ida. Thank you for the email. I was also very glad to have known you, and it makes me happy to think about the good times we had together. Wishing you all the best.

Love,
Hanne

Usually, we have to pull ourselves together to take care of what's nagging at us, but the reward can be a wonderful sense of relief as well as the feeling that you're in accord with your values.

Other times it may not be so simple to take care of such situations.

When the damage can't be repaired

My mother and I were alone when I was growing up, so we were very close. When she was old and sick, the nursing home called and said I needed to come if I wanted to be sure I was there when she died. At the time, I was in the middle of a conference I had arranged. I took a chance on her hanging on for one more day, or at least until I was done with my own presentation. It was as if I didn't really believe that this strong woman who had overcome so many challenges in her life could die. But when I got to the nursing home, it was too late. For a long time afterwards, I was tormented by guilt.

— Mads, age 58

A situation like this isn't easy to do something about. And it can be tempting to try to put it out of our minds. Such repression, however, carries much too high a price. We end up with less vitality and with losing contact with our own emotions.

The experience needs to be dealt with, even though it's painful. The more Mads allows it to be in his awareness, the quicker he will become accustomed to the emotions involved, and the easier it will be for him to endure them. We can deal with a failure like this in many ways. For example, we can write letters to the dead and say what we didn't get said. We can speak to many others about the experience if that's possible. Or seek professional help. Most clergymen, for example, are good to talk with about guilt.

All pain contains the potential for growth. Mads had always been considered a stern man. But after failing his mother, he became less harsh in judging others. His sternness had worried his mother. Now it was nice for Mads to think that if his mother was watching him from somewhere, she would be happy knowing he had used the pain he felt after her death to develop new, gentler sides to his personality.

Take note of how you talk to yourself

We've just seen how self-reproach, in some instances, can lead to something good. Other times it can rob you of your energy without benefiting anyone. That happens in particular when self-criticism is more or less an automatic reaction, and we're not fully aware of what's going on.

Often, we don't really hear the thoughts or dialogue going on inside us. When I explore this with a client in therapy, sometimes she's surprised to discover how she talks to herself. "You idiot," "Now you've screwed it up again!" or "You should've known better" are examples of unkind self-criticism.

If you want to discover your inner criticisms, you have to be particularly alert when you sense your mood plummeting or when you start feeling anxious. Ask yourself: "What was I thinking?" or "What did I tell myself right when I sensed my mood changing?" Be particularly alert to the word "should." For example, "I should have done that differently, I should be happier, more welcoming, smarter, friendlier…" or whatever it is you're demanding of yourself. We use the word "should" in our criticisms. We can direct them outside — "You should…" — or inside — "I should…"

If you haven't worked with yourself, you will probably talk to yourself in exactly the same way and in the same tone of voice your parents spoke to you when you were a child. If they were loving, you will talk to yourself in a loving way. If they were critical, you tend to criticise yourself.

Realising that you're attacking yourself is an important insight. It's necessary for being able to change the situation. To begin with, you need to find out if your self-criticism is constructive or if it's ruining your mood for no reason. If the latter, you need to set it aside and begin sending friendly messages to yourself.

Practice seeing yourself with friendly eyes

If you find you have a bad habit of criticising yourself for things you can't do anything about, you need to form a new habit to defeat the old.

Changing habits requires persistence over an extended period of time. One good method of training kindness to yourself is: Get a notebook to be used only for this training exercise. At least once a day, focus on the good or constructive things you've done and write them down in the notebook. See yourself the way the most loving father or mother would see their child. Even if your positive efforts didn't end up the way you wanted them to, acknowledge yourself for your good intentions. At least three things every day.

Maren wrote in her notebook:

This morning I woke up with this thought in my head that I would try to be friendly to my colleague. When I got to work, there wasn't really any opportunity, and besides that, I forgot my vow. But it was a good thought — and I'm glad I had it.

I took the stairway and walked all the way up to the fifth floor, even though I wanted to take the elevator. By doing so, I did something good for myself and for the climate.

I asked Jesper if he'd like to go out somewhere together. He didn't have any free days on his calendar, but it was brave of me to ask.

When you train a new habit, you should keep at it for at least three or four months. That's how long it takes for your brain to get used to a new way of doing things.

Exercise:

Be aware of your self-criticism. When you feel your mood darkening, you can catch a critical inner remark by asking yourself, "What just went through my head right then?" Write down what you were blaming yourself for.

If the message was to do something different from what you usually do or to make up for something you've said or done to someone, consider acting on it.

If you realise that criticism is only a bad habit, change the habit to something more constructive. Every day, write down in a notebook three things you've done or thought that you feel are praiseworthy. Do so every day for three or four months.

Summary of Chapter 2: Discover the message in the anger you turn inward

Anger turned inward can have positive as well as negative effects. The positive might, for example, be when the anger inside nudges you towards getting something important done. The negative can cause stress and depression. You might be overburdening yourself with criticism that robs you of your energy and sunny mood.

CHAPTER 3

Find out if the guilt truly is yours

Influence and guilt are connected. If you have no influence on a situation, it's not your fault if something goes wrong. For example, it's not your fault if your mother has problems because of a difficult childhood. Nor is it your fault if the firm you're working for is struggling with a deficit from before you were hired. Or if a storm ruins a plan to go sailing, you can't do anything about the weather.

It makes no sense to blame people for something on which they had no influence. The judicial system takes the same view.

Therefore, when you want to do something about your guilty conscience, the principal question is:

To what degree do I have an influence on the situation?

If you have a guilty conscience about a messy kitchen, the question is, have you been home so you could do something about it? If the answer is yes, your guilt is justified.

In Helene's case, it's not:

A year ago, stress got the best of me. I was on sick leave from work, but that's not all. I'd promised a friend I would help her, and I had to tell her I couldn't, and I also had to cancel attending a parent-teacher conference at my kids' school. My friend felt bad about me backing out, and the teacher told me it was a very important conference. It made me feel guilty, like I wasn't good enough.

When I answered the question about what influence I had on my situation, it was a relief to answer that it certainly wasn't my idea to get sick. It helped me realise it wasn't my fault, in spite of the disappointment of others around me.

— Helene, age 42

In addition to how much influence you've had on a situation, another important question is:

Am I the only one who had an influence?

Share your guilt

Maybe you actually have had an influence on a situation, but not to the degree you originally believed. Sometimes we take all the blame for something on which we've had only a partial influence. Or deny all blame, even though we actually did affect the situation.

When the atmosphere at a family birthday party becomes strained, it's seldom the fault of a single person. Everyone present has an influence on the mood in the room. Some people are quick to take the blame for this, while others immediately shun it.

It can be an enormous relief to go from "all of this is my fault" to "I'm one of many who are to blame for the way things are going."

An example:

Sofie's daughter Line was having a hard time learning to read. Sofie thought it was because she hadn't been practising enough with her daughter. Or that she was unable to make sure Line was happy and energetic and wanted to do the lessons. Sofie's self-criticism robbed her of the energy needed to help her daughter. While speaking with a psychotherapist, Sofie realised there were many factors involved in Line's problems with reading:

- Line's father let her get away with not doing her homework when she stayed with him.
- Sofie's parents were too busy with their own lives to get involved with their grandchild.
- The Danish teacher wasn't particularly good at teaching.
- Line's father had also had trouble learning to read, so her problems could be inherited from him.
- Sofie was tired when she got home from work, and she didn't always have the strength to make Line do her homework.

Sofie assigned percentages to how much each factor was involved, and it ended up looking like this:

- Genetic predisposition for reading difficulties: 30%
- Weak teacher: 30%
- Father allowing Line to not do her homework during the weekend: 10%
- No support from grandparents: 10%
- Sofie doesn't always force the issue about homework: 20%

Besides the list, she drew a pie; see below:

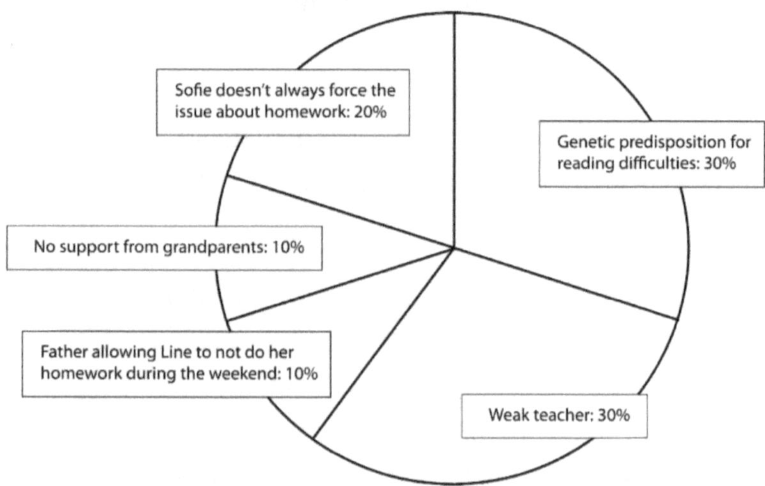

It became clear to Sofie that she wasn't the only one at fault. She was satisfied, though, with the 20%. 0% would have meant she had no influence on Line's reading skills, and she certainly didn't want to be that unimportant. On the other hand, putting all the blame on her shoulders was too heavy a burden. The pie exercise helped reduce her self-criticism and share the blame with others.

Later on, Sofie had a talk with Line's father about the importance of him taking an active part in Line's reading. She spoke to her parents about how vital their support was to her, so she wouldn't be solely responsible for so much. She contacted the school and managed to enrol Line in a group that received extra tutoring.

She now feels able to deal with her 20% of the blame. She has decided that on the days she's most tired, she will pick up Line at her after-school youth club an hour later than usual. That way, she can rest, after which she'll feel fresher and more able to take on the challenge of getting Line to do her homework.

Knowing that others also have reason to feel guilty helps Sofie in that now, she can share the blame. It's a great relief for her, and in addition, the others now have the opportunity to take more responsibility and help Line.

The positive benefits of sharing guilt with others

If you tire easily for no good reason, your feelings of guilt might be excessive. Perhaps all your self-criticism exhausts you, or you're demanding far too much of yourself. If you also blame yourself for your fatigue, if you believe it's all your fault, you're caught in a vicious circle.

One way to find out if too much criticism is being turned inward is by experimenting with directing more of it outward. Ask yourself: who else could be part of the problem? Make a list.

Martin was less energetic than his co-workers and his girlfriend. Much of the time, he felt inadequate and was unhappy that he didn't get more done. Martin made a list of those who had some influence on how tired he felt:

- My employer
- My girlfriend
- My doctor
- My parents
- My co-worker and friend

After you've made a list of your accomplices, write each one of them a letter. The letters are not to be sent to them; you're writing solely for your own benefit. Make it a game, don't worry about what they might think if they read the letters. Give each person some of the blame and responsibility for the problem. You can suggest to each of them how they could contribute to improving the situation.

Here are Martin's letters:

Dear Boss,

Haven't you seen how tired I look at the end of every day at work? Doesn't it make you think I might be doing too much? Or that I'm not getting enough recognition for what I accomplish? Have you thought about what you could do to help me be more energetic? If not, I suggest you start thinking about it.

Yours,
Martin

Dear Camilla,

Have you noticed how tired I look a lot of the time? What do you think you can do to help me feel more energetic? I need much more love, warmth, and sex. If we could start every day by making love, I'm sure I would have a lot more energy. But you probably don't want that. Have you thought about anything else you could do? Like, not being so annoyed about things I don't get done. Maybe you have some other suggestions. I think you should spend a little time thinking about your role in my fatigue.

Love,
Martin

Dear Doctor,

I've spoken with you about my fatigue several times. But all you do is take some blood tests and say there's nothing wrong. I don't think that's good enough. You need to do more. I want you to examine me thoroughly, find out what's wrong, and find a cure.

Yours, Martin

Dear Dad and Mom,

I wish you'd taught me how to lead a happy life.

Love,
Martin

Dear Hans,

Have you noticed how tired I look after we've been hanging out for several hours? Why don't you ask me why I look so tired? Or if there's something bothering me? You like telling me all kinds of things. Do you think I like listening to all of it? Because I don't, not all the time, Hans. I'd rather talk a little bit more about me.

Love,
Martin

It can be very energising to direct your anger outward. Even while he was writing, Martin could feel how the letters were relieving his guilty conscience. He realised he needed to move more in that direction, and he decided to talk to more people around him about his fatigue.

If you find you're too far on one side of the scale, it can be healthy to go too far to the other side to create balance. If you tend to turn all your anger inward and burden yourself with a guilty conscience, it's a good idea to do the opposite. Send the anger out. Do it in your mind, fantasise, or write letters you don't send, use them to explore how it feels to direct all of it outward. If you have taken on blame that belongs to others, it becomes too heavy a burden, and you get nothing out of the physical and mental resources the other guilty parties might have.

A very bad guilty conscience can also stem from strict principles that, for example, prevent you from setting limits. Read more about that in the next chapter.

Exercise:

Think about some event in your life you feel bad about that has given you a guilty conscience.

Besides yourself, who else had an influence on the situation?

Make a list.

Put a percentage on each person's share of the blame and make a blame pie.

Write a letter to each of them and tell them what they can do or stop doing to make you feel better. The letters are not to be sent to these people; they are for your sake only, to experience how it feels to assign some of your guilty feelings to others.

SUMMARY OF CHAPTER 3: Find out if the guilt truly is yours

The person in control of a situation bears the responsibility if something goes wrong. If you don't have influence, you are not to blame for what happened.

It's rare to be the only one at fault. Often, you're only an accomplice. It can be a relief to discover that instead of bearing 100% of the blame, you can share it with other people or other factors that influence the situation.

CHAPTER 4

Focus on your map and your basic principles

How well you feel you're doing in life is, of course, associated with your external circumstances and the challenges you meet. But your sense of success or failure depends even more on how you deal with your life situation.

An example:

Nikolaj has been denied public funding for his education. If he thinks, "My caseworker probably doesn't like me," he'll be unhappy. If he thinks, "I should have done a better job on my application," he'll be angry with himself. If he thinks, "They probably felt I have too much going for me," he'll gain a sense of determination and look for other possibilities.

Two people can experience a situation in two very different ways. How you respond to your opportunities in life depends on how you see the world and yourself. And the principles you live by. You can't always change your circumstances, but you can work on the way you deal with them as well as the expectations and standards you have for yourself and your life. Breaking off with overly rigid rules, outdated expectations, and ambitions that lead to guilt can be a source of great relief and gratification.

Your personal map

We all live according to a specific map that tells us what to expect and how to achieve a good life.

It's not at all certain you've given a lot of thought to the map that's guiding you. Maybe you've simply taken over your parents' map. If so, it's a good idea to give it a critical look. What kind of a map are you picturing in your head? What challenges and opportunities do you expect to meet in your life?

Excessive expectations can easily lead to a guilty conscience.

If you expect to be happy most of the time, you'll look for a reason when going through a boring or troubled period in your life. You might find the reason outside yourself and get mad at your partner, your parents, your job — whoever or whatever you think is to blame for your unhappiness. Or you might aim your anger at yourself: "There must be something wrong with me."

Imagine if someone at the beginning of your life had given you the following map detailing what you could expect:

- Hard work is a part of life. You don't always feel like doing it, but you have to anyway.
- You will be humiliated, you will face adversity and disaster, people will let you down and betray you, and once in a while, you won't live up to your own values.
- There will be quite a few bad days.

- During the last half of your life, your physical beauty will fade away.
- You will end up losing everything.
- But once in a while, you will experience joy, love, and intimacy with other people.
- There will be moments of special meaning.

If you're alert to making use of the opportunities for growth inherent in your adversities, you will experience the happiness that comes from overcoming challenges, maturing, increasing your insight, and being useful. And if you can avoid bitterness, as your physical capabilities wane, you may experience even more growth in your inner life as well as in your ability to love in an unselfish way.

Bad days are a part of it

Everyone goes through rough days. Some people won't accept that. They become angry and frustrated, and they blame the outside world:

"I deserve better."
"This isn't fair."

Others direct it all inside:

"I should be able to organise my life to avoid bad days."
"What am I doing wrong?"

Whether you direct your anger outward or inward, you risk digging yourself deeper into negativity. A rough day doesn't need to be someone's fault. It's all about not making it worse with negative or bitter thoughts.

Sad days can be used to reflect on things and to consider if there is something you can change or do better. Just be aware that if you start evaluating yourself on a bad day, it can easily deteriorate into brooding and self-recrimination. On a day when you just don't feel happy, it can be more productive to tell yourself one or more of the following:

- I guess this is one of those days I just have to get through. I'm going to be good to myself, and I'll look forward to better days.
- Pain in life is an opportunity for growth, to become more mature, and to carve out more room inside me for happiness.
- Today might be a special opportunity for growth.
- I'm going to spend the day training empathy with people who are doing badly — and with myself.
- It's always darkest before dawn. Maybe this day is the beginning of a new and deeper happiness.

If you change your expectations and your map to make room for bad days that aren't necessarily your own fault, it can ease your guilty conscience.

Examine your basic principles of life

Besides the laws and rules of society, everyone has basic personal principles they've either inherited from their parents or formed themselves and decided to live by. Most people aren't fully aware of the maxims they live by. Maybe you could benefit from taking a close look at yours.

Our basic principles in life are formed from good intentions. They regulate our behaviour in a way that is to our advantage. They can function as an inner guide to help us find the good in life.

When you examine your own principles, you might become aware that one or more of the guidelines you're living by are having the opposite effect of what was intended. A maxim such as "I may never say no to a friend in need" denies you of taking care of yourself. And "I will always look perfect" is a recipe for making your life difficult and exhausting yourself to no one's benefit. If you realise that one or more of your principles are doing more harm than good, you'll be very motivated to change them.

Maybe your basic principles come from your parents. Maybe you're living by maxims you came up with but now have forgotten. It's like eating with a spoon. If you haven't tried it before, it's hard to do: how much should you put in the spoon, how do you avoid spilling it on the way up, and how do you guide the spoon into your mouth? After we've learned, we never think about it, it's automatic, and we don't remember why we do it exactly the way we do.

You might not even be aware that you're living by principles formed when you were a kid, and today they are outmoded and damaging.

As I've written earlier, there are people who seldom have a guilty conscience. Others can feel guilty about the smallest mistake. If you're one of the former, your principles might be too lenient. If you're one of the latter, they might be too strict.

Examples of strict basic principles:

- I may not make mistakes.
- I must always give something of myself to others.
- I must never make another person unhappy.
- I have to ensure everyone around me is doing okay.
- I may not compare myself to others in a way that makes me look good, and I must definitely not be happy about it.
- I may not get annoyed with other people without a reason I can explain.
- I may not have expectations for others.
- I may not cause any problems for anyone.
- If someone gets mad at me, it's my responsibility to make sure the person will like me again.
- I must be friendly and always happy if someone knocks on my door.
- I must always be there for a friend in need.

How to discover principles that create guilt

The choices we make in life are often a compromise between what we want and the values and principles we try to live by. That's why our maxims become clearer when we have to make a decision. Questions such as, "Why don't you just do what you want to?" or "Why don't you just stop doing what you don't want to do?" will reveal principles as well as values. For example, "Why did I answer the phone when my mom called, even though I didn't feel like being interrupted?" Or "Why did I agree to do that extra work at my job, even though I know I'm going to pay for it because I'll be exhausted after work?"

The answers could look something like this:

- You may never say no to your parents.
- You must always be helpful.

You can also uncover a principle by paying attention to your self-criticism or by focusing when you sense a feeling of inadequacy. Try to catch the thought linked to that feeling. What did you say to yourself at that moment?

When I realise that a decision I made has consequences I don't like, I get really mad at myself. I've discovered I have a rule that forbids me to make bad decisions. After I wrote it down and sat and thought about it, it was clear to me how much depressing self-criticism it creates.

— Eva, 29 years old

Everyone makes bad decisions. You can't predict the future, and you can't calculate all the consequences of the choices you make. Often you discover them many years later. At the moment you make your decision, there can be a frightening number of unknown factors. It can't always end well. Sometimes you'll discover later on that it would have been better if you'd chosen differently. When Eva realised she was demanding something impossible of herself, she got rid of the rule. She wrote down with a magic marker: "Everyone makes a bad decision once in a while." She stuck the message up on her refrigerator. Besides cutting down on her self-recriminations, she felt less anxious about making decisions.

The stricter your principles are, the more difficult it is for you to live up to them, and the greater the risk of being the victim of your own anger. This is why a close examination of your basic principles can be extremely beneficial.

When you've discovered your principles, write down the pros and cons of each one on two separate sheets of paper. Later you will see that some of them are working fine, while others are creating more problems than they solve.

How to adjust your principles

Sometimes all you need to do is reformulate an inapt rule just a bit to cut down on your guilt and self-criticism.

Here are several examples:

I discovered that one of the rules I'm living by leads to self-criticism almost every day. It was: "I have to keep my weight below 80 kg." Most of the time, I weighed about 84 kg, and I was always fighting myself to get my weight down.

After I thought about it for a while, I decided to raise my limit to 84. And now I'm a lot less critical of myself because of my weight.

— Erik, 47 years old

When I changed the principle "I will always do my best at work" to "Most of the time, I'll do my best, but on days when I'm tired and feeling run down, it's okay to do just enough to get by," it made me a lot happier to go to work.

— Margrethe, 27 years old

One of the most stressful principles I discovered was "I always have to be there for my friends." It was a problem whenever my friend called, and I didn't want to talk on the phone. I'd barely even noticed I was annoyed before answering in a friendly voice. I don't like being irritated, and I would try to ignore it. I felt I should be happy she called. I was always tired afterwards.

I decided to make a new rule: "When one of my friends calls, I don't absolutely have to answer. It's okay, as long as I get back to them within a day." I wrote down the new rule and hung it up on my fridge, so I'm reminded of it often.

— Anna, 19 years old

Anna doesn't like her annoyance, and she ends up turning it inward. It becomes self-criticism, which creates a sense of guilt. It's a quick and effective way to lose all your energy.

When you want to change one of your principles, it's very much worth putting extra effort into it by not only composing the new principles in your head but also writing them down on paper and reading them over and over. If you don't like to write, try saying them out loud several times.

While you're training a new principle, shut down the old one. You do that simply by breaking it. The more you violate your principles, the less power they have over you.

Break your undesirable principles

Principles are linked to presumptions about the world. For example, if one of your principles is that the needs of others are more important than your own, it might be connected to the presumption that you aren't particularly important.

If it's difficult for you to break the principles you want to get rid of, it's a good idea to take a good look at the associated presumption. You can find that out by asking:

- Why should I…?
- What will happen if I don't?
- Why must I not…?

When Anna asked herself why she always had to be there for her friends, at first, she couldn't find the answer. It had always been that way for her, an absolute given. Her mother had always been available, answered the phone, and opened the door with a smile when somebody wanted her for something. When asked what would happen if she didn't answer the phone, at first, Anna said her friend would be angry. But then she recalled that her friend didn't always answer her phone. And when that happened, it didn't really bother Anna because she knew her friend would call back.

After this little exercise, Anna was ready to reformulate that principle in her life.

When you dare do something different — or don't do something you've done for many years, possibly your entire life — it will often be associated with uneasiness or anxiety.

The first time Anna let her phone ring, she felt bad about it. She felt like a lousy person. But after she'd practised doing it several times, it seemed more natural to her. Over time she stopped thinking so much about it; she enjoyed her new freedom to not have a conversation she didn't feel like having.

Living by a new principle demands a lot of attention at first. If you're under pressure or scared or simply tired, it's easy to revert to the old maxims you've perhaps been following your entire life. It takes less energy to follow old principles that are practically reflexes than to pull yourself together and do something different. There's absolutely no reason, though, to lose heart when you do experience a relapse. It's completely normal, and in time it will happen less often if you keep following your new principle and remind yourself about it at every opportunity. You can tape a copy of it up on a mirror or someplace where you'll see it frequently, or you can tell a friend about it and ask her to remind you of it occasionally.

If you loosen up your principles to make it easier to live up to them, you can cut down on your feelings of guilt.

Making changes in yourself will always be connected with fear, however. Read more about this in the next chapter.

Exercise:

Think about your ideas and expectations for your life. Talk to other people about them and consider whether or not they are realistic.

Focus on your basic principles. You can discover them by asking yourself why you choose the way you do, especially when you decide to do something different from what you actually want to do.

Write down your basic principles and reach a decision about each one.

Do any of them often make you feel guilty?

Could there be advantages to relaxing any of them?

Summary of Chapter 4: Focus on your map and your basic principles

Thoughts and basic principles have a great influence on how often you experience feelings of guilt and how strong they are. If you have high expectations for happiness and success in life, it will be easy to blame yourself or others when life doesn't live up to them. Fine-tuning your expectations can lessen your feelings of inadequacy.

If you live by strict principles and believe you should be almost perfect at everything, you risk burdening yourself with a guilty conscience strong enough to rob you of your energy.

If you focus on your thoughts and principles, you'll discover that small adjustments can make a big difference and that you will feel less guilt and more vitality in your life.

CHAPTER 5

Don't allow your fear to control you

Fear is part of a guilty conscience. If you are very afraid of anger or of being rejected, you will easily become a slave to others' expectations. You can end up on a hamster wheel. No matter how hard you try, no matter how fast you run, occasionally, someone will criticise you. If you're all too eager to please, you risk annoying people. Doing everything possible to be a good person can end up with others feeling inferior to you and bad about themselves, and they might develop a negative attitude. Besides, people who like to criticise others will do so, and they will always find something to fault, no matter how much you try to avoid it.

Be friends with your fear

You can work with a bad conscience the same way as with anxiety in cognitive therapy: expose yourself to what you fear. If you're afraid to ride an elevator, that's exactly what you should do until you've done it enough that you feel safe.

If you're scared of a specific emotion, you'll probably do everything you can to avoid situations where it appears. If you hate having a guilty conscience, you're apt to do more for others than you have the energy for. And people around you might simply raise their expectations, giving you less and less time for yourself.

If you instead go the other way and cut down on your helpfulness, you'll feel your guilty conscience; that's when the opportunity arises to practice hanging out with it. Be curious and inquisitive about the feeling and remind yourself it's not dangerous. You can train your ability to endure a feeling the same way you train a muscle. The more work you put in, the better you become at it. And eventually, the people around you will expect less of you.

An example:

I've been plagued by stress, and I know I have to take care of myself. But when my sister calls and needs someone to look after her kids, I can't say no. If I did, I would feel so guilty that my day would be ruined anyway.

— Helle, 42 years old

What she's overlooking is that her guilty conscience will recede if she trains being in its company without acting on it immediately. The third time she says no to taking care of the kids and instead goes for a walk outside and relaxes; she's become so used to the guilty conscience that, in spite of it, she enjoys her free time.

Feelings of guilt can crop up in many different situations. Often, they appear when we choose not to live up to someone else's expectations or values.

An example:

____

It's always been important to my dad that I get an education. Textbooks have never interested me, and I've never wanted a job where you just sit in front of a computer screen. When we have a family dinner, and my cousins get all this praise for their long, complex educations, sometimes I glance over at my dad. It makes me feel terrible to see how sad he looks.

— Kasper, age 32

____

Kasper chooses to go his own way instead of living up to his father's expectations. When he sees his father is sad about not being able to celebrate a degree like others in the family do, he feels guilty, and in fact, he's thought about getting some sort of short education just so his father has something to tell when his friends ask about his son.

His guilt is rational in a way. Kasper is in fact the reason why his father is sad once in a while. But the responsibility is on the wrong shoulders. It's not Kasper's job to make sure his father has something to brag about to his family and friends. It's his father's responsibility to lead his own life in a way he's proud of. And it's up to Kasper to be true to himself (which is important), even though he feels guilty about it because of his father. Psychotherapist Bent Falk calls this form of guilt "existential tax." It's the price you sometimes pay for being true to yourself.

Learn to accommodate your emotions

Some children grow up with parents who help them learn to endure the anger or disappointment of others. Parents who support them in their right to have the emotions they have. It's not strange that these children become robust and tolerant.

Others grow up in a family where the parents have problems with their own emotions, and they react to their children's emotions in a way that makes the children feel they are flawed or unloved. If you are one of the latter, you probably have problems with wholeheartedly accepting yourself and your emotions. Maybe you occasionally feel your emotions make such a ruckus inside you that it's difficult to go through with something, even though you know it's the best thing to do. If, for example, you can't stand making your child unhappy, you may not be able to set the necessary boundaries for them, which can end up with your child acting in a way nobody cares for. If you can't stand it when your partner gets sad or angry, you risk being stuck in people-pleaser behaviour, which is basically devoid of intimacy and good contact between you and your partner.

It can be tempting to keep others at a distance when you're trying to avoid a guilty conscience. You wouldn't feel guilty on a deserted island. With more remote relationships, such as a neighbour or a supermarket cashier, it's relatively easy to behave correctly and avoid guilt. But in close, meaningful relationships, in addition to making the person happy, once in a while, you're going to make them unhappy, too. It can't be avoided. The more important you are to someone, the deeper their disappointment will be when you don't live up to their expectations. And the guiltier you will feel. If it's difficult for you to handle feelings of guilt, the problem will be particularly serious in relation to someone who means a lot to you. Fortunately, there are other solutions to this problem besides isolating yourself.

If you train and become good at enduring unpleasant emotions, you'll be more comfortable in your relationships. And you'll be able to give yourself time to gather yourself and decide how to act on your emotion. Sometimes you might choose to apologise and offer to make it up to the person. Other times you might say to yourself: "I'm going to consider my bad conscience as an existential tax as the price I have to pay for something like having the weekend all to myself." Hopefully, you'll feel the weekend was worth it, despite your bad conscience. And maybe you can feel good about having the courage to make a choice that at the time was unpopular with someone but, in the long run, proved to be a good thing for others because your free weekend allowed you to recharge your batteries.

Find the courage to be unpopular

Sometimes making a choice that at the time pleases everyone can later have unfortunate consequences, while making an unpopular choice can, in the long run, be what's best for most of those involved. If, for example, you ignore your own needs to meet those of another, you'll be popular. But the risk is great that later on, you will want to break off the relationship. If you prioritise your own needs half the time, the chances are much greater that the relationship will be good for both of you, also in the long run.

Another example might be if you let your child have the candy she spots at the supermarket checkout. You'll be popular with your child, as well as the cashier. But you'll probably be more satisfied with yourself in the long run if you say no. And while you feel guilty because your child is screaming, which annoys the cashier and everyone else in line, notice also how much you grow and mature as you stand by your decision, even though you're isolated. You might realise that the problem isn't the guilt you're feeling but everything you've done to avoid it.

Exercise:

Focus on your fear of your own or others' anger or opinion. Be curious and inquisitive about this fear. In which situations does it become serious, and in which is it a minor concern?

Experiment with following your own values, even when others around you don't like them. You can take small steps at first, for example, by expressing your opinion even though you know it might be unpopular. If someone reacts in a negative way, take a deep breath, sense how you feel, and try to endure the uneasy feeling without immediately trying to smooth things over with excuses or explanations.

Summary of Chapter 5: Don't allow your fear to control you

A bad conscience often contains a great deal of fear for your own or others' anger or opinions. The fear can push you to great lengths to live up to everyone's expectations, which will satisfy no one. But no matter how hard you try, there will always be someone who wants something more out of you. In addition, you run a serious risk of burning out and developing stress.

Instead, be friends with your fear, train yourself to be able to handle your bad conscience without immediately acting upon it, isolating yourself, or in any other way struggling to make it disappear.

CHAPTER 6

Expose a lack of responsibility

If you often develop a guilty conscience, you attract people who shun responsibility and will gladly give you all the blame. That's why it's important to be able to spot a lack of a sense of responsibility in people, to prevent yourself from being trapped in a relationship where you compensate for the other person's absence of initiative or drive.

It's not that some people are generally overly responsible, while others always take on too little of it. Often a person has some areas where she takes a lot of responsibility, while in other areas or periods in life, she's not up to it.

A lack of responsibility can be the result of low self-confidence. When my father was reluctant to get involved with my siblings and me, I think it was because he felt my mother was much better at it, and he was unsure how he could contribute. On the other hand, he was very responsible when it came to our family's economy.

Just as people can show various degrees of responsibility in different areas, different people can be responsible to a greater or lesser degree.

A description of the most extreme form of a lack of responsibility follows. It crops up when we see ourselves solely as a victim.

The problem with seeing yourself as a victim

Sometimes we see ourselves as victims of other people's unkindness. It's a way of seeing the world, where we place everything bad outside ourselves. In that position, we feel ourselves to be innocent and mistreated and, in all likelihood, also helpless and vulnerable. Maybe we direct our anger towards certain people. This is the ultimate disavowal of responsibility.

Seeing ourselves as a victim can mirror our actual reality. Sometimes we're ambushed by adversity we can do nothing about. It could be illness, death, robbery, etc.

It could also be harassment at work or physical or emotional violence.

It's not coincidental who gets victimised by violence or harassment. But it can be a positive trait that sets off the harassment of the victim, such as talent or high ethical standards.

Of course, true victims do exist. But when we consider ourselves innocent victims and all the trouble as something that comes from the outside only, most of the time, it's because we're unconscious of the part we play.

The following is not relevant to true victims. It's a description of what happens when we, or someone close to us, fall into the role of a victim.

An example:

Maria felt mistreated by her adult children. When she thought about how much she'd done for them, she felt it was totally unreasonable that they only visited her a few times a year. She thought they were egotistical, and she was angry about it. When Maria had guests, she spoke bitterly of her ungrateful children.

Maria considers herself to be an innocent victim and is completely unaware of the ways she could change the situation. For example, she could:

- Try to find ways to be more attractive to her children.
- Find other people to be with.
- Find a hobby to occupy her time.
- Seek help to break out of her negative thoughts.

Maria thinks that if she's going to get better, her children will have to change their ways. This is a complete shunning of responsibility.

Children can be the victims of adults they are dependent on. They don't have the same degree of opportunity adults have to make decisions that can improve a situation. Once you become an adult, you're being unrealistic if you consider yourself helpless. Adults who deny all personal responsibility and give others the blame create enormous problems, both for themselves and for others. Not because they're bad people but because they're trapped in a damaging pattern of behaviour and haven't put the past behind them. It's likely that a childhood trauma led to their strategy of playing the victim, a trauma too devastating for them to deal with. One they, therefore, have partially or even completely repressed.

It's not that certain people always take on the role of victim while others never do. Most of us can fall into that trap when under enough pressure.

The victim trap

There are people who consciously portray themselves as victims in an attempt to manipulate, grab power, or demean their foes. But usually, the person in the role of victim is ensnared by her pattern of behaviour and automatically shrinks inside, becomes small when she can't handle challenges and is fed up with herself, or when her anxiety becomes too much for her.

Falling into the role of a victim can be a defence against a reality you can't endure. Once in a while, after a sudden death, the person left behind becomes very angry at those she believes are to blame for the death. It could be a doctor or hospital personnel who weren't quick enough. Or the minister, who is sometimes considered to be God's representative. The widow experiences herself or her spouse as a victim of other people's mistakes or lack of responsibility, and they lash out in rage. If the person is relatively healthy emotionally, this condition will pass when the shock fades, the grief process starts up, and space for her own emotions begins opening up.

To understand the mechanism of victimhood, try to recall situations where you've experienced it in your own life. Maybe you've seen yourself as a victim of the world's evil, if only temporarily, when for example, you got an unexpected bill, experienced rejection, was shocked at someone's anger, or were given a job you couldn't handle.

An example from my own life:

Once when I was a pastor in Djursland, Denmark, I saw myself as a victim. I felt I was being harassed by the parish church council. I sensed that my female friends were growing tired of listening to my complaints and appeals for help. Clearly, they didn't know what to do. I felt terrible and didn't dare make the necessary decisions. I didn't even dare acknowledge I had a choice.

Only several years later, at a distance from the situation, did I see that I hadn't been easy to negotiate with either and that there was a structural problem in the national church that none of us could be blamed for.

As long as you're trapped in the role of victim, you see the world in black-and-white, and you most likely have little desire to put yourself in someone else's shoes. Sometimes getting away from the situation is enough to develop a more nuanced understanding of it.

The unresolved emotions from childhood

Most likely, an adult stuck in the role of the victim has genuinely been a victim as a child. Anger doesn't come from nowhere. There has been a situation in the past where the emotions were appropriate.

An example:

Inger said that her mother had threatened to kill herself, which is why as a ten-year-old, she'd panicked if she couldn't find her mother when she came home from school. But it seemed as if Inger was divorced from her emotions back then. She insisted she'd had good parents and a good childhood.

In her adult life, she constantly fell into the role of victim. For example, she would be convinced that a workman had cheated her. She tried to get everyone around her to hate the workman, and if she'd had the power to ruin him professionally, she would have. That's how enraged she was.

As a child, Inger hadn't been able to accommodate the anxiety and anger that was a natural reaction to her situation. Back then, no adult had helped Inger deal with her emotions, to lead her to see and feel the reality of her situation.

With the help of a therapist, as an adult, she could have worked with those past emotions and gained better contact with her present emotions. Maybe she didn't have the necessary courage or emotional strength for that. Now she dumps the repressed anger from her childhood onto others, not realising she involves others in a game that has very little to do with the here and now. For her, it's very real that others are evil and out to get her.

Exercise:

Think about a time in your life when you thought of yourself as a victim. Consider whether you truly were a victim or if you'd had options you overlooked.

Summary of Chapter 6: Expose a lack of responsibility

The problem in giving others the blame is that we do nothing to remedy the situation when often we are the only ones who can.

The ultimate in shunning responsibility is when we see ourselves solely as a victim. We might have been just that — when we were young and dependent on adults. When as adults we see ourselves that way, most likely, we *are* victims — but only of our own negative patterns and irresponsibility with regards to doing something about them.

CHAPTER 7

Be aware of regression

When we take on the role of victim, we more or less lose contact with our adult self and its capabilities. In psychotherapy, we call this regression. Regression is falling back to an earlier stage of development. A child who has been potty trained, for example, may start wetting herself when under stress, such as when a little sister or brother comes along or when she starts kindergarten. And a grown woman otherwise adept at communicating and negotiating may cry like a little girl if the intensity of her anger scares her or if she can't deal with the challenges she faces.

If you're overly responsible and easily form a guilty conscience, you're a prime candidate to take on the role of enabler for a person showing signs of regression. The overly responsible and the insufficiently responsible make a perfect fit. This is why you should be particularly alert, so you don't lock someone into a state of regression by taking over.

To understand the mechanisms of regression, as you read the following section, try to recall situations where you yourself were regressive. It probably doesn't happen often, but you might have experienced something that can lead you to a deeper understanding of what it's about.

The good regression

All of us occasionally need to let go of acting like an adult and being in control of everything. In a good relationship or friendship, you can switch off, letting the other party regress. When you run into problems you can't immediately handle, for example, it can be a great relief to let go for a while, to not have to take care of anything, just cry, be a little kid again, while someone listens and perhaps holds you. It's a form of caring that can re-energise you and give you the courage to meet the challenges life holds.

Regression is only undesirable if you don't come out of it fairly quickly, back into your adult self, so you can act and make necessary decisions.

When regression becomes a problem

When you're regressive, you're hoping someone will help you out of the situation you're in. Maybe you've just momentarily forgotten everything you can do, the ways you can help yourself.

An example:

One evening, when I was already stressed out, I got my finger caught in a door that I'd slammed shut a bit too hard. I wasn't sure if I should go to the emergency room, so I called my boyfriend. He didn't answer or call back. I became more and more frustrated and annoyed when he still didn't call. I paced the room and looked at my watch the whole time. I felt I'd been let down, and I called again and cried as I left a message that ended with, "What the hell do you think you're doing?" Then I cried and cried and cried.

Finally, three hours later, he called. He'd been home, but he'd forgotten his phone was on mute. He promised to come over as soon as he could.

After I talked to him, I calmed down. I was a little bit embarrassed about my reaction, and I wondered why I hadn't thought about calling someone else, reading on the net, or taking a picture of my finger and sending it to my sister, who is a nurse. There were lots of things I could have done, but it was like I'd slid down into a hole and couldn't see out. I felt so helpless without my boyfriend.

— Maren, age 27

Taking on the role of a victim is a special form of impotent, regressive rage with the power of a very hungry infant. The person feels like a helpless, innocent victim whose troubles have been caused by others.

How to escape the victim trap

As mentioned, a victim is in a regressive state. When you feel you're a victim, for some period of time, you've probably overlooked the capabilities and choices you have as an adult. Most likely, anxiety is making you feel like a little girl or boy inside. You need to get back to your adult self.

This exercise can help you do that. Think of situations where you faced enormous challenges. Write them down on a list and answer the following questions:

- How did I handle the challenge?
- What abilities did I use?

I came up with this exercise one evening when I realised I was the only one who could check a rat trap the next morning. I sat curled up on the sofa with a lump in my throat, thinking of all the stories I'd heard in my life about rats in traps that weren't quite dead, that were maimed and crawling around. I thought, *I'm not going out in the back hallway tomorrow morning. I can't, I simply can't.*

Fortunately, I knew this anti-regression method and started thinking about the challenges I'd met in my life. I thought about the time I had drifted too far out in the Atlantic. I swam against the current and towards the shore for all I was worth, even though my body began to ache, and for a while, it looked like I was getting nowhere. Then I thought about the time I hit another car, and the passengers jumped out and stared angrily at me. I hated to get out of my car, but I did it anyway. Lastly, I thought about the birth of one of my children when there were complications. After those memories, I was able to remind myself that I was in fact persistent and good at pulling myself together to do what had to be done, even though it was an awful situation.

I began thinking again about the problem facing me. I sat up straight on the sofa and realised I could deal with the next morning's challenge. Of course I could.

The pride and happiness I felt after carrying the dead rat out to the trash were indescribable. Usually, when we break out of our regression and do something about our problem, a reward awaits us.

How you can help someone else out of the role of victim

If the person stuck in victimhood is a close friend or in your family, you should help her out of her regression. Ask her what challenges in life she has handled before, or remind her of the ones you know about. For example, "Do you remember when you got fired, and you two almost had to sell the house? That must have been an incredibly tough time for you. How did you handle it? You must be a really strong person, don't you think?"

You're not helping by listening to her complain about other people, especially if you're confirming that she has reason to be angry. She'd love to hear you say something like, "That's just so unbelievable," or, "He ought to be ashamed of himself." It would definitely make her happy and contribute to a good atmosphere — though only in the short run. In the long run, it's unhealthy for both of you because you're helping her to hold onto a game that belongs in the past. It's much more productive to offer to talk to her about what options she has to make the situation better.

If she seems open to it, you could also talk to her about back when she truly was a victim, when she was a child. If she works on the wounds from her childhood and makes room for the emotions from back then, she'll no longer need to continue playing her game with people.

It's not at all sure, though, that she is motivated to escape her quagmire. There might be too many advantages to seeing herself as an innocent victim, or perhaps she is too afraid.

If that's the case, your job is to take care of yourself.

Exercise

Think about situations where you have been regressive. Consider if you lost contact with your adult self and your possibilities to act, or if they had been short, healthy periods of regression.

Make a list of challenges you've overcome. Put the list some-place easy for you to access. It could be helpful the next time you run into a problem that seems impossible to solve.

Summary of Chapter 7: Be aware of regression

There is such a thing as a healthy regression, which is part of receiving comfort from someone. It lasts only a short time and can be a much-needed release. If the regression drags on, it creates a problem both for the person experiencing it and often for those closest to her.

You're not helping someone who is regressive by agreeing with her complaints about others. She needs to get out of the regression and back into her adult self, so she can begin to take responsibility and solve her problems.

Should she not be motivated to put her regression behind her, it's important for you as a friend or family member to watch out for yourself.

CHAPTER 8

Set limits

Let's return to the example in the last chapter involving Inger. In many situations, she acted like a victim of workmen, doctors, the bureaucracy, or others she felt had treated her badly.

Inger's daughter, Josefine, couldn't avoid being dragged into her mother's conflicts. Inger's anger had a frightening force because it came from her childhood, where she had felt her life was in danger. Whenever there was a conflict, her emotions filled the entire room.

When she was a child and teenager, Josefine did everything she could to help and support her mother in her battle against "evil people." She was deathly afraid of her mother putting her in that role. She'd experienced it a few times, such as at a dance recital when she was wearing a beautiful dress her mother had sewn, and she wet herself. Her mother was furious and felt that Josefine had ruined the day for her and had taken away all the joy of sewing the dress and showing it off. Josefine felt so ashamed that she wanted to disappear from the face of the Earth.

Inger saw herself solely as a good person who, time and time again, was the victim of others' wrongdoing. As a child, Josefine accepted her mother's self-image without question. It caused her serious problems. You can only have positive feelings for a beautiful, innocent person. Josefine tried to dismiss her feelings, but inside she felt unreal and all wrong.

Victims demand self-repression

Inger insisted on something that only small children can expect: that everyone around her set aside their own emotions and needs. Maybe you've been around a child in distress, and you instinctively forget yourself and focus all your attention on caring for the child. The same can happen when you see a troubled adult. The problem is if it keeps on happening. Or if you aren't aware of the mechanisms involved and you act reflexively whenever you see someone in need, or even maybe when someone just looks a bit tired.

Probably without being aware of it, an adult in regression will appeal to the people around her and try to make them want to put her needs foremost. Her plea is difficult to see through. She sends out signals on a childish level, often only non-verbally. It can be a whiny tone of voice or a desperate look. You might feel the same urge to help as you would if she were a child, yet at the same time, you might feel yourself resist because something is wrong. At first, you might not understand the problem: she's an adult who is trying to wrest something out of you that only feels natural to give to a child. At least if it goes on for more than a short period of time.

Being in the presence of the victim doesn't allow you a broad palette of emotions. The victim insists on being treated only in a positive way. The annoyance and frustration arising naturally in you are given no room. If you don't see through the act, you can easily direct your irritation back at yourself and feel guilty and all wrong.

Set limits for what you will listen to

A person who basically is enraged and thinks only in black-and-white can be extremely stressful to listen to. A self-righteous rage can be intense, and if you are very close to the person, it can get under your skin.

Inger's daughter says:

When my mother was enraged at someone or the other who'd mistreated her, just talking to her on the phone made me flip out myself. One day I was sitting at work, I'd just hung up after talking to her, and a colleague burst into the office to ask me about something. I heard how incredibly irritated I sounded when I answered her, and she looked frightened. And I was frightened myself. That's not how I usually talk to my colleagues. But it was as if my mother's anger had crept into my system.

— Josefine, age 44

After a period when Josefine didn't feel at all like answering when Inger called, she managed to tell her mother how stressful it was listening to her anger. Josefine added that she wanted to talk to her if they could just agree that from now on, her mother wouldn't bring up all her conflicts, and they would talk about something else. At first, her mother was angry and felt betrayed. But she realised she would have to go along with her daughter if she wanted to keep their relationship intact.

The victim's anger

The anger of a person in the role of the victim can be so forceful that she loses all empathy for whoever she's angry at. She's very unlikely to be interested in seeing things from the other person's side. Often, she's not aware of how angry she is. She might think she simply feels bad and all the aggression is coming from someone else.

It can be difficult for family or loved ones to see through a victim's false sorrow.

When I was a child, I thought my mother was sad. That's what she said. And it made me feel twice as guilty if she was angry about something I'd done. Because it was really too bad for Mom that she felt sad. Only when I was past the age of thirty did I begin to understand that what she called "sad" was in fact rage. That's when several pieces fell into place for me.

— Josefine, age 44

If you begin to see that the person is actually angry, it will be easier to allow yourself your own anger and set limits.

Exercise:

Think about how you typically react when you're listening to a person complain about other people, a person who looks on herself as solely a victim. Do you fall into the victim trap with her, or do you talk to her about possible ways she could change her situation?

Summary of Chapter 8: Set limits

If you are close to someone who sees herself as a victim, it's especially important that you look out for yourself. The person might not be aware of how strongly she's appealing to you to take over. You might feel guilty about her unhappy situation, or that you don't always feel the emotions she needs, or that you can't help. It's important to be very clear about your limits, that you are the one who decides how much you will listen to and how seriously you want to get involved.

CHAPTER 9

Acknowledge your guilt

The moon has a dark side hidden from us. We do, too, even though we're not always conscious of it. Bad qualities do much more damage when they are concealed. It's important for us to bring them to light and make peace with ourselves.

In the previous chapter, we went over how to protect yourself when you're close to a person who lacks responsibility. This chapter is about how you can become more whole by taking ownership of all of your characteristics, including those you don't care for. The more whole you are, the easier you can protect yourself against the untethered guilt often floating around in groups, waiting for a chance to land.

You can utilise your annoyance with others to uncover the parts of yourself you're unaware of. The next time a person does something that offends you, say to yourself out loud, "That's something I might have done, too."

An example:

I absolutely couldn't stand it when I heard people snapping at each other. When I told myself, "I could have done that too, on a day when I was under a lot of pressure," not only did I sense it was true, but I also felt like snapping at several people I know. The exercise helped me see people in a more favourable light. I also decided to cut myself some slack about behaving less than ideal now and then.

— Poul, age 32

If you see yourself as "right," failure or wrongdoing will be something only others are involved in. It could be said that you're getting others to bear some of your dark side. The more you're able to integrate your less endearing qualities, the more clearly you'll be able to see and have room for others. And the more whole you will be. The pathway leading out of victim mentality goes through becoming aware of your dark side.

Growth and maturity come from realising how much we have in common with other people, including those we don't like. The more we grow out of our urge to judge others, the less harshly we judge ourselves.

If you want to be true to yourself, you need help from your dark side.

If you have chosen unconsciously to identify only with positive qualities, such as friendliness and gentleness, while repressing the more confrontational and blunt sides of yourself, it becomes difficult to make an unpopular choice. If you dare to identify occasionally with being egotistical or helpless, it will be easier to carve out a place for yourself in the world and to live your life the way you truly wish to.

Take responsibility for your choices

Acknowledging negative feelings such as annoyance or envy makes it easier to control them and keep them from holding sway over you. And you'll also avoid being afraid of such emotions when you spot them in others.

Standing up for yourself in your entirety, for your dark sides as well as the lighter ones, allows you to create a space where others find the courage to do the same. Being honest about your own inadequacies can be catching, the result being that an atmosphere of openness and acceptance spreads around you. In the opposite case, for example, if a mistake or an accident happens that no one wants to take responsibility for, the mood in the family or group will often become tense. If one person dares stand up and say, "It was my fault," the mood will lighten considerably.

By acknowledging your mistake or your guilt, you avoid others taking it on themselves. The following is an example of how honesty about choices and responsibilities in a divorce can relieve children of guilt they are too young to bear.

Mette had decided to get divorced. "Otherwise, I would be depressed," she told her friends, her husband, and her children. It was a good explanation, and it absolved her from a heavy load of guilt. But her children seemed unhappy and troubled, and they wouldn't talk about it. Following the advice of a psychotherapist, she chose to be clear and direct about her decision.

She told the children, "I know you're unhappy that I'm breaking our family up, and I can understand if you're angry and think I've made a selfish decision."

After a moment of total silence, she added, "I wish I could have gotten the life I want without you having to pay. I hope someday you can forgive me."

It had taken Mette a long time to pull herself together to tell them this. The result was worth it. It became easier to get her children to talk about the divorce. Her contact with them improved, and she was happy for the opportunity to help them unburden themselves.

When Mette explained that she had to get a divorce, that otherwise she would be depressed, she lightened her own guilty conscience. But the children, on the other hand, felt guilty about their sorrow and anger. They couldn't allow themselves to react in a negative way if their mother really didn't have a choice; they couldn't allow themselves to burden her if she was a helpless victim.

We all have our reasons for choosing the way we do. When we take on guilt without drowning others in self-justifying explanations, begging for forgiveness, or in some way putting others in a difficult situation, the damage we cause them is held to a minimum.

Give a gift

If you choose to take on guilt, you will probably ease someone else's shame and feelings of wrongdoing while increasing their happiness and quality of life. We become wiser with time. You've probably looked in the rear-view mirror and had to admit that because of a lack of insight, you acted in a way that hurt someone.

An example:

____

When my kids were little, I was angry at my husband because I didn't feel he did his share of the housework. He had just started his first job as a teacher. Maybe I was also a bit jealous that he got out of the house and could talk to other adults. I didn't feel he had any reason to complain about the new job being hard. I had seen my sister's husband get home from work and put on an apron and get started. I felt he was being incredibly unfair, and I yelled at him about it and insulted him. We ended up getting divorced.

Ten years later, I got my first teaching job and discovered how hard it is to teach. Also, I had gained a greater understanding of how people are different and that not everyone has the same energy level. I was embarrassed about how I had behaved.

— Majken, age 52

____

Once in a while, we all have to acknowledge, as Majken did above, that we've been too quick to judge someone wrongly. Often, we don't take the consequences and go to the wronged person and make up for it.

____

Majken did:

Twelve years later, I contacted my ex-husband and suggested we meet for a cup of coffee and talk about the old days. When we got together, I told him I was sorry I had yelled at him and made him appear wrong and that now I could see he'd been doing his best. He responded by saying that he could certainly understand it had been hard for me, being home with the kids. We had a good talk about being young parents, and we were even able to laugh a bit about our mistakes and how naïve we were.

____

A meeting like this, where condescending remarks are taken back, can have enormous meaning for both parties. In the example above, as long as nothing is done, the offending remark will probably still be nagging at him and can be a factor if he has low self-esteem. Taking the blame for something can be a gift that means a great deal, and it doesn't cost much at all.

Exercise:

Think back to a situation where you've judged someone. Consider whether it's possible you yourself have the characteristic you condemned. Maybe it's one of the qualities you need to master to solve one of your problems.

Think back to a situation where you definitely were at fault. Say to yourself out loud: "It was my fault." You could even write a letter to the person wronged and take the blame. Think about whether anyone around you needs to hear you say that something was your fault. If you end up saying it to the person, you've given them a gift, and in all likelihood, the other person will be relieved and happy to hear you say it.

Summary of Chapter 9: Acknowledge your guilt

Accepting and standing up for ourselves and the complexity of emotions, desires, and thoughts we all have is something we need to train our entire lives. The better we are at it, the less we will project our own emotions or qualities onto others. And the better we will be at bearing our guilt without falling into damaging patterns of behaviour that, in turn, lead us to either burden ourselves with even more — and excessive — guilt or to deny it and pass it onto others.

CHAPTER 10

Avoid compensating

Guilt is so difficult for some people to handle that they try to escape it through various strategies of compensation. It can be a person who feels she's not particularly attractive and therefore tries to compensate by being extra friendly or helpful. Or it might be a case of actual guilt — something a person has done and regretted and is trying to make up for. The problem arises if the person continues to compensate over a long period of time, to where it almost becomes a lifestyle.

Three examples follow: a parent's relationship with her adult child, a relationship between two brothers, and a woman's relationship with her mother.

Example 1: A parent compensates in relation to an adult child

My daughter, Louise, is twenty-five years old now and still hasn't settled into a permanent relationship. I'm worried that she might have been impaired by my not being particularly caring and loving when she was young. Intimacy has never been my strong suit. I'm energetic and effective, and I'm at my best when I have lots to do. Nowadays, I drop everything when Louise needs my help.

— Anna, age 53

____

Anna's guilty conscience about her intimacy deficit when Louise was young is causing her to compensate by being overly helpful and dropping everything the second Louise needs her. When Anna showed up at my office, we spoke about her guilty conscience, which she often tormented herself with. I asked Anna how caring her own mother had been when she was young. It was an eye-opener for Anna to realise that her mother and grandmother also had shown a lack of intimacy, that it was a family problem. Now she could share her guilt with the other women in her family. It was a relief.

Anna's guilty conscience isn't the real problem here. It says something about her, namely that she wishes she could have done better. It would have been much worse if she simply didn't care. A guilty conscience that you've learned to give space to and live with in your life matures your personality to the degree that not many other challenges can. The strategies of compensation Anna has been utilising are a much greater problem. The message they send to Louise is that Louise's problems are her mother's responsibility. Taking away responsibility from others isn't healthy for anyone, including our adult children. It's vitally important that they, not their parents, are responsible for their well-being in life.

Louise is a grown woman now, and as such, she is the only one who can make a life she's proud of living. No matter how much Anna wants to, she can't do it for her. Louise's childhood wounds provide an opportunity for her to grow. Only she can transform the pain into gain and make a life for herself she's happy with.

As a parent, we can help and support our adult children and even offer to pay for psychotherapy if we can afford to, if we believe it can help. But we have to hold ourselves back and allow them to go through their own crises, make their own choices, incur their own guilt, and take responsibility for it.

Looking on passively while all this is happening is easier said than done. The yearning to carry our children on our backs through the difficult times of life can be enormous, and the pain of witnessing their failures can be almost unbearable. But the reward for not overly involving ourselves in our children's lives is to watch how they grow, to see their happiness and pride at meeting and conquering a challenge.

Instead of becoming too involved in our adult children's lives, it's better that we concentrate on being good role models.

Besides going to therapy, Anna worked on her capacity for intimacy by practising yoga and meditation. To begin with, she did so to show the way for her daughter, who also had problems with intimacy. Later it became a new lifestyle for Anna; she began to enjoy her life in a new way. At the same time, she prepared herself to be a loving, caring grandmother should she one day be given the opportunity.

It's difficult to give our children more than we've received ourselves. Every family has its own challenges, large or small. Some families have problems with abuse, others suffer from serious conflicts, and still, others are prone to anxiety or depression. Talents and problems are passed down through generations. As far as the latter goes, you can work on halting a negative inheritance by going into therapy and improving yourself, for example. If you manage to pass something on that is just a bit better than what you received, you're making a positive contribution. If you expect to be the perfect parent for your children, despite a serious family problem weighing you down, you're demanding too much of yourself and risk being paralyzed by a bad conscience.

Example 2: Birgitte compensates because of guilt about an undesirable emotion

My mother has had practically no schooling. I have an advanced degree. When my mother expresses her rash opinions, they sound stupid to me, and I get annoyed. And I get mad at myself about that. She's not to blame for her lack of education. When I'm with her, I've noticed that I put on a smile every time she looks at me.

— Birgitte, age 37

If Birgitte had dared to stand up for her feelings and dropped the smile, it would have been much less of a strain for her to be with her mother. And her mother would probably have been more at ease by not being met with a big false smile. Her mother might initially have felt bad to learn that her opinions made her daughter want to roll her eyes. But that's how it was, and it was much better to deal with that than to try to create or maintain an illusion of something different. Helping others maintain their illusions about themselves takes a lot of energy, as well as being a waste.

Example 3: Hans compensates because of something bad in his past

I picked on my little brother, Per, when we were kids. Per had a lot of problems as a teenager, and he thinks it's from being bullied. He's also had problems as an adult, and he keeps a distance to me.

Of course I'm sorry about the way I behaved and the problems he has because of me. Every time I see my brother or hear about his problems, I cringe. When I'm with him, I do all I can to make things nice for him. I listen to his problems and try to help, but he almost never follows my advice.

After a weekend with Per, I often have the empty feeling of having wasted my energy.

— Hans, age 62

No matter how much Hans apologises or compensates, he can't change what happened. By taking responsibility for Per's well-being today, he does more harm than good. The only one who can bear that responsibility is Per.

If Hans expresses his powerlessness instead of trying to please his little brother in every way, he'll be more in line with the reality of the situation. He could say, for example, "I wish I could go back and do it over again."

We can have various reasons for feeling we should sacrifice our own happiness to be there for someone else. But when we do, we end up placing a burden on the person we want to help; it becomes their fault that we're not living our life to the fullest. Of course, we can pretend we enjoy sacrificing ourselves. By doing so, we fool them — and possibly even ourselves — into believing something that isn't true and that seldom turns out well in the long run.

Forgive yourself

A guilty conscience is anger turned inward. It makes sense when anger can pressure us into doing something important. For example, to keep the promises we make to ourselves or others. But in situations where we can't or don't want to change something, inward-turned anger can be a complete waste of energy.

If you fail to meet the needs of those closest to you, criticising yourself doesn't help. It makes no sense to do so, either, because you don't choose your limitations. Besides, it's no catastrophe if a loved one faces extra challenges because of your inadequacy. Nobody gets to live a life without problems. And challenges can be transformed into growth.

We all make mistakes and bad choices, and we all learn from them along the way. We have to try to make peace with ourselves and the choices we've made.

Sometimes self-recrimination is pure self-punishment. It can serve as a defence against facing something unpleasant. For example, what's done is done, and it can't be changed. That I'm the reason something bad happened to myself or someone else. That apparently, I'm not as good a person as I thought I was. There can be a lot of guilt to swallow before we're able to lower our defences and forgive ourselves.

Most likely, you did your best, from what you knew at the time. If you look in the rear-view mirror and clearly see that you acted entirely egotistically and perhaps even against your own values, acknowledge yourself for having the courage to admit and accept your guilt. Don't give yourself a life sentence. If your guilt is too difficult to live with, find someone you can talk to about it.

Forgiving yourself doesn't necessarily mean you're no longer aggravated with yourself. You don't have full control over your emotions. To forgive can be to decide to stop punishing yourself and instead do your best to focus on the positive.

Exercise:

Think about if you have one or more relationships where you pressure yourself to give more than you actually can because you're trying to compensate for something you've said, done, or felt.

Summary of Chapter 10: Avoid compensating

Some people try to rid themselves of a bad conscience by compensating for the wrong they believe they've done. Maybe they punish themselves for life. That's not a healthy strategy, however. What's done is done, and no one can undo it, no matter how much they compensate.

If you sacrifice yourself in a relationship to atone for a wrongdoing, the relationship won't be authentic. And you risk taking responsibility from that person, who is the only one able to transform their pain into growth and do what's necessary to move on.

Making up for something can be a good solution as long as you don't bind yourself to a long-term period of self-oppression, which does no one any good.

It's important to forgive yourself.

CHAPTER 11

Get rid of irrational feelings of guilt

A bit further on, I will show you how to work with irrational guilt. First, however, I will make clear how that form of guilt differs from both rational guilt and shame.

The difference between guilt and shame

A basic difference between guilt and shame:

- Guilt is about *doing*. About something you have or haven't done.
- Shame is about *being*. About something connected with your person that feels embarrassing or wrong.

There is a reason involved in guilt. If you feel guilty, usually you can explain what you have or haven't done that caused something bad to happen. Shame is different. Typically it's a vague feeling of being so wrong that it's embarrassing if anyone discovers it. You can be ashamed about something involving your appearance; for example, if your hair is very thin or if you discover you spilt sauce on your shirt. You can also be ashamed of something you want to do or of a feeling you think is embarrassing — falling in love with someone you have no chance with, for example. The truth is you can be ashamed of all sorts of things. Often, it's about emotions or characteristics that others have a hard time seeing as embarrassing.

What we become ashamed of varies from individual to individual. One person can be ashamed of her love, while the other can be ashamed of her anger. You can also experience shame without being able to pinpoint exactly what it is about yourself that feels so shameful and wrong.

In the case of guilt, our focus is on the damage done; typically, instead of the embarrassment connected with shame, we feel a need to act.

Seldom do we turn to specific self-recriminations when feeling shame, except in a situation where we feel we should have been better at concealing it.

Shame can't be made up for. And neither is there an urge to act, except for wanting to run away and hide.

Irrational guilt

This form differs from rational guilt in that it's out of proportion to the influence you have. Feeling guilty is irrational when it's about something you have no control over. For example, you may feel guilty about being born if your mother had to marry someone she otherwise wouldn't have. Or if you are born with the "wrong" gender, not the one your parents wished for. Or because your emotions aren't what your partner or child needs.

Your guilt is irrational because you can't be guilty of something you have no control over. You don't decide how you feel about someone or whether you were born as a male or female.

Irrational guilt can resemble shame. You're sure you're doing something wrong, but you're not sure what it is or what you can do to make up for it. The feeling that you should be doing something else is likely based on the illusion that you have more control of or influence on the situation than you actually do.

An example:

When I visit Dad, a lot of the time, he's focused on giving me advice about my life. It's obvious he's not doing very well, so I try to be kind to him, even though I don't care for his advice. I'm always working overtime in my head to figure out how to start a constructive conversation with him.

When I leave, he always thinks it's too early, "you just got here," he's always saying. On the train going home, I feel like all my happiness has disappeared. I'm tired and sad, and it just seems so difficult to deal with anything. I feel guilty about my father not doing well, and I can't seem to help him.

When I got home the other day, my girlfriend said, "You're doing your best, Rune. No one can ask for more than that." Then I cried, and I could feel how hard it had been. It was like a lump in my chest broke up, and there was room enough in there to feel happy again.

— Rune, age 42

It can seem strange that you have the urge to act when feeling irrational guilt, even though you typically have no idea what to do. That's exactly what makes the situation so distressing and sad.

Rune blamed himself for not being able to make his father feel better. Earlier, it had felt as if his self-criticism was forcing him out of his own body, it had been that severe, and he was beside himself for several days. But gradually, he learned how to let his sweet, wise girlfriend help him, so he relatively quickly felt like himself again.

In many situations, the question of whether your guilty conscience is rational or irrational can't be answered with yes or no. Often there is a kernel of rational guilt that grows out of proportion to where your bad conscience worsens. For example, you break up with your partner, and later on, he begins to fall apart. If you think his problems are all your fault, your bad conscience will become too severe. You may be partly to blame, but a divorce is never only one person's fault. How well he gets along is primarily his own responsibility.

Irrational guilt must be uncovered, so it's clear to you how much out of proportion it is to your situation. When you finally understand it's irrational, you can examine it and be curious about it. Why did it become so dominating? What do you have at stake that's being threatened? The following two exercises can help you explore the situation.

Examine your guilty conscience

Irrational feelings of inadequacy or guilt can be difficult to uncover. A letter of apology can help you come closer, so you can better see what's going on.

When you write the letter, let go of your rational self. Who cares if what you're apologising for is even anyone's fault? Who cares if it makes any sense? Simply let your guilty conscience try to redeem itself by apologising. Allow it to speak freely with no censorship.

An example:

One day Henrik's ex-girlfriend stopped by. She was still wild about him, and she'd spent considerable time on her appearance and brought along a great meal. She patched a hole in his pants and did everything she could to make him feel good. When she left, in addition to being exhausted, he had a bad conscience.

This is his letter of apology:

> *I'm sorry that I'm not just as crazy about you.*
> *I'm sorry for being bored while we were together.*
> *I'm sorry I'm not in love with you anymore.*
> *I'm sorry that you're wasting your time.*
> *I'm sorry that I'm happy, even though you're not.*

After writing the letter, Henrik could see that his guilty conscience was way over in the red on the irrational meter and that he couldn't help not having the feelings his ex-girlfriend had been appealing to.

Express your powerlessness

We can express powerlessness by using the expression "I wish."
It was a relief to Henrik when he rephrased his letter:

I wish I was just as crazy about you as you are about me.
I wish I had been cheered up and inspired.
I wish I could make you happy by being in love with you, too.
I wish I could give you a future with me.
I wish we both could be happy.

One more example:

Eva has been to a family birthday party. She wasn't in the mood
for it, and her sister seemed a bit distant towards her when they
said goodbye. When she got home, she felt like a failure.

Here is the letter of apology she wrote:

I'm sorry I was tired.
I'm sorry I didn't get around to talking to everyone.
I'm sorry I sat around in a daze some of the time.
I'm sorry I wasn't happy and fun.
I'm sorry I thought a lot of the talking going on was uninspiring.
I'm sorry I couldn't lighten the mood.

Later on, she changed it into a letter of powerlessness:

I wish I'd had more energy.
I wish I'd spoken to everyone.
I wish I'd been able to be more alert and attentive.

I wish I could have made everybody laugh.

I wish I'd felt more inspired.

I wish I could have spread joy among everyone there.

Love, Eva

After she'd written the second letter, she could give herself credit for her good intentions, and she felt better.

Here's another tool for examining and dealing with irrational guilt.

Let your guilty conscience speak

Write a letter to yourself from the point of view of your feelings of guilt. Let them tell you what you should do to make them feel okay with the situation. Let them give you their message. Karoline imagined herself to be her guilty conscience, and she wrote:

Dear Karoline,

Stop rejecting him. You can see it makes him feel bad. He needs you to be there for him. Think about how lonely and abandoned he might feel. You simply have to love him more. He's doing everything he can for you. Give him more of the good sides of yourself. You owe him that. You have to make sure he's happy all the time. He deserves it.

Best,

Karoline's guilty conscience

After you write the letter, write up a list of its claims. Karoline's list:

I should love him as much as he loves me.
He deserves to be loved.
I should be there for him.
I have to make him happy.
Instead, I make him feel bad.
He deserves the best.

After she'd let her guilty conscience speak, it became obvious to her that the demands she'd listed would be better suited for an all-powerful God than a mortal human being.

When you've made your list, answer every single point with an argument that refutes it.

Karoline answered this way:

You can't decide for yourself how much you love another person.
You can't deserve to be loved.
Everyone needs time for themselves, where they aren't at anyone's disposal.
He's the one who has to manage his life in a way that makes him happy. It's no one else's responsibility.
It doesn't hurt anyone to be sad.
No human being is so good that they deserve to never face hardships or disappointments. We all have to live with pain in our lives, and pain is often a door to new opportunities.
Let him have his hardships and defeats in peace so he can grow strong.

By doing this exercise, Karoline realised the enormity and impossibility of the demands she'd been making on herself. This insight broke the power of the negative thoughts swimming around in her head and gave room for other, more creative thoughts.

It's important that you not only do the exercise in your head. Your thoughts need to be written down, so you can see them from the outside. Buy a standard-size notebook with blank paper, no lines or squares. Allow your guilty conscience to speak on the left side and answer it on the right side, so you can see your guilt and your answer to your guilt side by side.

Sometimes your emotions tell you something different from your rational thoughts. For example, you can have a very bad conscience after a meeting that turned into a fiasco, even though you knew you did your best. Or you can feel guilty about a traffic accident, even though you were hit from behind and had no chance of avoiding it. On the one side is what your head knows, while on the other side is what your emotions are telling you. Both messages can influence you and tug you in different directions. Or they might take turns being the dominant message. Seeing them side by side on paper makes any conflict between them so obvious that the wrong one has to yield.

When you finish writing the exercise in your notebook, sit down and take turns reading the two sides. Let your eyes move back and forth between them. Take your time and think about their differences, feel how that affects your guilty conscience.

Leave the book open somewhere you often walk by, so you'll be reminded that your guilty thoughts don't ring true. You can use the notebook every time you feel guilty.

If it's difficult for you to answer your guilt, it might be a good idea to talk to somebody about it. It's easier for someone completely outside the situation to get an overview of what's going on.

Maybe you can also find help in the box below, where you can read several examples of what is *not* your fault and one example of what could be your obligation.

What is *not* your fault:

That you have the emotions you have

You don't owe anyone certain emotions. Not even if they have the 100% correct emotions in relation to you. We can't choose our emotions.

That another adult is living an unsatisfactory life

Every adult is responsible for making a happy life for themselves. And for turning adversity into growth.

No one can demand a life without challenges, no matter how perfect a person they are and no matter how much of a pity it is.

That you have limitations

You don't owe anyone to do more than you can.

No one can demand that you love everyone around you unconditionally or that you give your children everything you never had, for example.

What you can be obliged to do

You can be obliged to do your best and to seek help when you fall short and your problems harm others.

In the next chapter, you can read more about irrational guilt and how it can be understood and dealt with.

Exercise:

Think of a situation that has given you a guilty conscience.

Write a letter of apology, say you're sorry about everything — including what is completely impossible and unfair. Then use the phrase "I wish" to change each apology into an expression of powerlessness. Take note of what it does to your mood.

You can also think of another situation and allow your guilty conscience to express itself in a letter to you. Make a list of the letter's demands or claims and respond to each of them. Write down your responses as well as the demands and claims and lay them out so you can see both sides.

Summary of Chapter 11: Get rid of irrational feelings of guilt

Sometimes the guilty conscience we feel is much stronger than the situation calls for. Irrational feelings of guilt reveal themselves when we ask them what it will take to get them to let up on us. When you realise how irrational they are, you can slip their bonds.

CHAPTER 12

Find release on a deeper level

If your guilty conscience is irrational, it can be a sign of something going on behind the scenes. Your feelings of guilt might be covering up a reality you're not confronting or feelings such as anger, powerlessness, or sorrow. It can also be a defence against acknowledging happiness you feel is wrong.

Guilt about happiness

A guilty conscience can be excessive because it's covering up a pleasure so forbidden that you might not even have acknowledged it. For example, you might feel happy about being more beautiful, richer, smarter, healthier, or in some other way better off than someone else. Some people feel terrible about being happy when they compare themselves to others because they mistake happiness for *schadenfreude*. But they might just be feeling grateful. And even if it is *schadenfreude*, at least it's a pleasure that doesn't hurt anyone — unless you feel you have to tell the world about it.

It's difficult to control your emotions, which is why even though you might want to, you can't make your happiness disappear. It's much easier to do something about your guilt. A simple solution could be adjusting your personal rule that, for example, forbids you to enjoy comparing yourself to others.

Anger as a cover-up emotion

Often it happens that after a loved one dies, a person becomes angry. The anger can be understood as a sign of crisis. In a way, the person is beside herself and unprepared to face reality, or she lacks the capacity for her emotional reaction.

If she is the type who directs her anger outward, she will point it towards those she believes are to blame for the death, such as doctors, nurses, or a slow ambulance. If there are no guilty parties, she might direct her anger towards the deceased or the family and loved ones she believes weren't around enough when the deceased was ill.

If, instead, she turns her anger inward, it becomes guilt and a bad conscience. It might be focused on the days leading up to the death when she wished she had done more or been there more. Or it might be about her relationship with the deceased, where she thinks she should have said more nice things, done more good for them.

Wherever the anger is directed, it can be seen as a defence against confronting reality. As long as your thoughts are focused on the past, perhaps on fantasies of how things could have been better, the death won't feel quite so real. You can momentarily delude yourself into thinking that all your anger or regret can change reality.

When feelings of guilt function as a defence, the one left behind isn't interested in being talked out of her anger or bad conscience. It can be difficult for the people around her to understand why she feels so guilty about words or actions that, from where they stand, seem normal. Seeing regret as a defence against other emotions or against facing a frightening reality can make sense out of everything. Only after a period of time, when the widow begins to feel like herself again, can she grasp that no one is perfect and that her actions and behaviour were human and forgivable.

The same mechanism can occur during other losses, such as losing a partner by divorce, losing friends, a job, or your health. Also, in these cases, a bad conscience can cover you like a heavy blanket, protecting against insights or emotions you aren't ready to acknowledge or don't have the capacity for.

Guilty conscience as a defence against powerlessness and grief

In the last chapter, I wrote about Rune, who feels guilty because his father is doing badly. Other emotions are probably hidden underneath. Annoyance with his father for giving him unwanted advice must be buried somewhere. Perhaps together with feeling so much sorrow from not getting what he needed from a father.

His guilt is anger turned inward. And there is a certain logic in Rune directing towards himself his anger over the dysfunctional contact with his father. It makes sense to be angry with whoever is the strongest, the one you believe has the power to change things. Perhaps Rune is subconsciously aware that he is stronger and more able than his father. Yet he overestimates his powers by thinking he can save his father. It's impossible to save anyone who doesn't genuinely want to be saved. Rune's father has no desire to change. He prefers to be the boss and give advice to his son.

Rune's guilty conscience is based on the illusion that he can change the situation. It's difficult for him to see the hopelessness in his father's circumstances and to witness his father's pain. He deeply wants his father to be doing well, and he has a hard time letting go of the hope that he can save him. But it's the illusion that he can and should help his father that's torturing him. It would be better if he directed some of his anger outward and used it to set limits for the unwanted advice his father gives him.

If you notice feelings of guilt in a relationship, it can be helpful to check for something you're not facing or acknowledging. If the other person in a relationship is doing badly and lacks the energy to be actively interested in you, you're probably feeling anger and sorrow just underneath the surface.

What you want is vital

It's important to know what you want in your relationships. Our emotions are reactions to whether or not our desires are being met.

If you are getting what you want, you'll feel happy.

If you think you can get it by fighting for it, your anger will rise along with your will to fight.

If you give up on what you want, sorrow will begin nagging at you.

If you're not ready to confront your reality and sense your grief or fighting spirit, guilt, and a bad conscience may have crept in over you like a heavy fog.

The first step out of the fog is discovering what you want.

You can search for what you want in a relationship by doing the following small exercise:

Write a letter to yourself from the person your guilt is focused on. Let the letter contain everything you fervently wish to hear from that person. Give your imagination free rein, no matter what objections your reasoning powers come up with. It doesn't matter if it's realistic. Try to dig deep inside yourself and sense what's there. What could the other person say that would make you happy and satisfied?

Rune wrote the following letter:

Dear Rune,

I enjoyed your visit. Thank you for coming by, even though I know you have a lot of things to take care of. Your visit warmed my heart, and that's something that will last a long time.

I'm proud and happy to have a son who's doing as well as you are. I know your life is tough once in a while. If there's anything I can help you with, be sure to let me know.

Love,
Dad

It became obvious to Rune how deeply he wanted his father to be happy, grateful, proud of his son, and feel well.

Find out what you can change

When you find out what you want, you've reached a very important crossroads. You might recognise this wise prayer of unknown origin:

> *God grant me the serenity to accept what I cannot change,*
> *the courage to change the things I can,*
> *and the wisdom to know the difference.*

Knowing the difference between what can be changed and what should be accepted as your circumstances can be difficult when you're in the middle of everything, with your emotions and desires all tangled up. Getting some distance from the situation can help you judge it.

Imagine you're a policeman. Ask yourself:

- What are the arguments for it being something you can change?
- What are the arguments against it?

Ignore your emotions and hunches. That's what a policeman would do. They can be influenced too much by what you want.

The questions and answers must be 100% concrete. For example, Rune could ask himself:

- How long has my father been doing badly?
- Has he ever been a completely well-functioning individual?
- Are there others who have tried to help him?
- Did they succeed?
- Was he grateful?
- Does he say he wants help or that he wants to grow as a human being?
- Is there anything that points to him not wanting to change?

Make up your own concrete cross-examination relevant to your situation.

Write down your answers.

When you try to see things from the outside, it can clear things up for you.

If you end up realising your relationship or situation isn't going to change, you'll feel sorrow. Then it becomes a matter of crying and getting it out and moving on. And while you're mourning, your guilty conscience will disappear. What you wanted won't go away. Your wishes are a part of who you are, and it's important you acknowledge them and look upon them with friendly eyes — also when they aren't granted.

There's nothing wrong with wishes. They are full of life. If you stand by them, as well as your sorrow at not getting what you want, you will avoid feelings of guilt and shame. You'll still feel the wish, and you'll be sorry you can't have it. But there's a big difference between fighting for what you want in hopes of changing something and throwing in the towel and instead using your energy on something else. The former is like knocking on a door that's been bricked up and blaming yourself for the door not opening. The latter is like turning around and seeing doors that might already be open a crack.

Sometimes it's all about accepting your situation and giving up not what you wish for but the hope of it ever happening. Other times we surrender too quickly and would be well served by taking up the fight again.

When you give up too soon

Not only can you waste opportunities by hoping for something you're better off dropping; the opposite can also be true.

Line gave up on an education that might not have been all that unrealistic if only she'd sought help to believe in herself a bit more. And Mads abandoned his quest to find a girlfriend before he'd checked out every possibility. Some people give up too easily. If you're one of them, you need to follow a different path, one that leads to fighting for what you want.

One of the balances in life is knowing when to fight and when to let go. If you're flexible enough, you'll find out that the balance tips back and forth continuously. One moment you're better off walking away, while the next moment, something shows up that you have to fight for.

Typically you're better at one than the other. If you're a fighter, a bulldog who never gives up, you need to train yourself to let go — and experience the relief that can follow.

Exercise:

Think of a relationship where you have a bad conscience. Consider whether or not there is something you're not facing or if there are other emotions hidden under your guilt.

Is it possible there's something you're angry about?

Something you miss?

Or maybe a forbidden pleasure?

Find out what you want in a relationship by writing a letter from the other person to you, in which they say everything you would love to hear them say. Make room for your sorrow if you realise you're not going to get what you want. Otherwise, maybe you should get fighting mad and go for it.

Summary of Chapter 12: Find release on a deeper level

If your guilt is out of proportion to the situation you're in, it might be covering up anger, a forbidden pleasure, a sense of powerlessness, or sorrow you're not yet prepared to face.

It's important to distinguish between what can be changed and what you're better off accepting. If you fight to change something that can't be changed, you risk turning your anger on yourself.

CHAPTER 13

Let go of an illusion of control

When you give up hope of getting something you want, it can be a relief as well as a misery. Sorrow brings out the caring in other people, and when you have finished grieving, you're ready to move on to new possibilities. If you enter your sorrow, your guilty conscience fades and often vanishes completely.

An example:

When I began to realise my sister and I can never again be as close as we were when we were kids, I was overcome with sorrow. My sister had been like a mother to me, she was the rock in my world, and I felt I could be 100% myself with her.

I can hardly stand how her husband, and now her children too, take up most of her life. I've tried every kind of way to please my sister in hopes of being important to her again — and I've been mad at myself for failing.

Most of the time now, I'm aware that I have to face up to my loss. But when my sorrow gets to be too much, I set it aside and fantasise about what I can do so we're close again. On the other hand, I feel like I'm putting a lot of pressure on myself — and I end up with a bad conscience. When I give up hope again and tell myself, "It's not going to happen, Ida dear, and it's not your fault," the sorrow returns with a vengeance. But then I feel more relaxed, feel better about myself.

— Ida, age 32

Some people fight far too long. As psychotherapist Bent Falk put it: "Those who are strong suffer the most. It takes them much too long to throw the towel in the ring." The strong persist in fighting far longer than what they have the strength and energy for.

Ida is a strong-willed woman who doesn't give up easily. She's taken many a beating and has suffered loss after loss, after which she blames herself. Yet she continued to fight for years before she finally reached the point where she could acknowledge her defeat.

We all know what it's like to refuse to give up a fight, even though it's costing us dearly, and even though somewhere inside, we know it's a lost cause. Giving up often demands that we also let go of an illusion of control.

Responsibility and control

The more responsibility or guilt we take on, the more influence we believe we have. And there can be a form of security in that. If it's your fault that you and your partner's relationship is going badly, you're also the one who can decide to change for the better for the sake of your relationship. If it's not your fault, then you can't save it. You have no influence over which way it goes.

Children readily take on much more of the blame for something than they realistically have. They overestimate their influence. The professional term for this is omnipotence.

It takes a long time for some of us to grow out of the omnipotent ideas about our importance, control, and influence. We take on the responsibility and blame ourselves for much more than we have control over.

An example:

I went out on a date with a woman I was head over heels in love with. She was everything I'd ever dreamed about: beautiful, charming, intelligent, and funny. We quickly became intimate, and everything was like the most fantastic dream — until three weeks later, she suddenly stopped answering her phone.

I was crushed. I paced back and forth in my apartment and couldn't get myself settled down. I sobbed while I went through every last thing I'd said to her and regretted all of it. One thing sounded totally stupid, and the other sounded self-centred. I put everything under the microscope and criticised the hell out of it. Agreed with myself that the worst was probably that I went way too fast for her. So I decided to give her some space and then contact her later on.

A year later, in a roundabout way, I found out that she'd never intended for anything between us to be more than a short fling.

— Lars, age 38

Lars immediately took full responsibility for her leaving. That's typical for when we find ourselves in a situation that takes an unexpected and unpleasant turn. As long as we take on all the blame, we can continue believing we have the power to change the situation.

It took Lars several months to stop his self-recriminations and realise there was nothing he could do; she didn't want to see him again.

The next example is from my own life.

As I explained earlier, for many years, I struggled with guilt in my relationship with my mother. The reason for my guilty conscience was an illusion of control. My hope was that if I did everything right, I could get my mother to change into an emotionally healthy, warm person, one who could actually see me and have room for me inside her. For several decades I blamed myself, until one day, I managed to let go of hope and the illusion of control and instead sense my sorrow and helplessness. Only then did my feelings of guilt loosen their hold on me.

Overestimating your abilities to overcome life's challenges can be very painful, as the examples above show.

Now I can see the comedy in how I took on so much more responsibility and blame than I had control over. That was quite an overestimation of my powers! Like when a small dachshund attacks a German Shepherd and gets beat up because it didn't realise it had bitten off a whole lot more than it could chew.

It's taken me many years to be able to laugh at what I thought I could accomplish. As I began to realise I didn't control nearly as much as I'd assumed, I felt a myriad of emotions — not the least of which was anxiety. The way to tackle that is to speak to someone about it. At least it goes faster than if you deal with it alone.

When we dare face our impotence and learn to accommodate the insecurity and sorrow it involves, a great reward awaits us: we stop speculating about guilt and torturing ourselves with a bad conscience.

In Africa, people catch monkeys by setting out a box full of nuts. The opening is so small that the monkey can barely stick its hand inside. And when the monkey grabs the nuts, its fist is too big to get out of the box, which is tied to the ground. The monkey is stuck. We can get caught in an exhausting struggle the same way because we're holding onto far too much. Sometimes the path to freedom is to let go.

Let your anger become sorrow

Anger is a type of fighter energy. Sometimes you use it to fight yourself. A fight that can end with stress and depression.

If you face up to your personal losses, you can grieve over them. And grief can bring you peace. Tears encourage the loving support of others. When you dare share your feelings in connection with a loss, it can bring out a great deal of love and deep intimacy.

You can help transform your anger into sorrow by writing a letter of farewell to what you have lost. Perhaps it is only a hope or dream. Several examples follow, but first, a few instructions:

Reach deep inside yourself and imagine what you wanted the very most, then say goodbye to having it. "Thanks" is always an important word in a farewell. If you can find something you can thank, it will help you let go.

Here is Rune's farewell letter:

Dear dream of having a warm, close father with lots of time and energy for me,

I thought I was the one who could and should make sure I got you.

It was too big a burden for me to bear, and I felt like a loser.

Overestimating myself might even have saved my emotional health.

It gave me hope. Thanks for that.

But it also gave me such intense feelings of guilt that I almost went down with the ship.

Goodbye, dream. And thanks for your company.

Goodbye to my hope of seeing my father become a happy man.

Goodbye to the dream of how wonderful we would have gotten along when I'd learned to do the right things.

Goodbye to feeling full of life from being with a warm, close father.

Goodbye to feeling my old man sees me and has room for me in his life.

Goodbye to what I never had and never will have.

Now I'm going to stop pulling on a door that never can be opened, and I'm going to turn around so I can see the doors that can.

Love, Rune

Below is an example of a farewell letter to something a bit more concrete, an education that was running Jørgen into the ground.

Dear dream of getting an academic education,

You will never happen. I see that now. But I've enjoyed fantasising about how wonderful my life was going to be when I finished my studies.

Despite everything, thank you for the good times I had while studying and for what I learned.

Now I'm letting go of you.

Goodbye to getting an academic education. Goodbye to all my fantasies and dreams about how I was going to celebrate my degree.

Goodbye to how I imagine myself having a master's degree.

Goodbye to all the admiration I'd been looking forward to.

Goodbye to seeing how proud my parents would have been.

I've enjoyed all these dreams. Goodbye, and thanks to all of you.

I thank myself for taking the chance and for trying.

When I finish crying, I'm sure I'll find another education I can cope with better.

Love,

Jørgen

When we let go of a struggle, we can put a lot of our guilty conscience and self-recriminations behind us.

Another example:

Sidsel was constantly at odds with herself about her weight. She thought she had too much fat around her waist, exactly as her mother had. When she was younger, she was contemptuous of her mother for not staying on a diet to rid herself of her rolls of fat. But after Sidsel had children, she ran into exactly the same problem, and she was mad at herself. Her letter:

Dear dream of being as thin as a model,

I'm letting you go now.

Goodbye to the hope that someday I could get into the pants I bought before I had kids.

Goodbye to thinking I was better than my mother.

Goodbye to the hope of getting my weight down to where I wanted it.

Goodbye to the dreams of looking at myself in the mirror and enjoying the sight of the thin woman there.

Goodbye to the self-confidence I imagined a slim body would give me.

Now I'm going to go out and find my self-confidence and self-esteem somewhere else.

Sincerely yours,
Sidsel

When Sidsel let go of her struggle to be thin, she also got rid of many feelings of failure, inadequacy, and guilt.

Exercise:

Think of situations that have given you a guilty conscience.

Consider whether there is something you can let go of. A hope, or something you're struggling with yourself about.

If you manage to find one, write a farewell letter and experience your guilty conscience changing into sorrow.

Summary of Chapter 13: Let go of an illusion of control

It can be a relief to realise there are limits to your influence and what you can control. Letting go of what you want can sometimes be exactly what it takes to abandon a fight and find peace of mind.

AFTERWORD

Kindness spreads

Exaggerated guilt is a torment you put yourself through for no good reason. I hope you are able to use the tools in this book to cut down on feelings of guilt out of proportion to your situation.

Your rational guilt is a fact, and your guilty feelings in that regard are a healthy reaction that should be taken seriously. Looking at yourself with friendly eyes is not the same as ignoring your slip-ups and dumb mistakes. It's important to face up to reality. Personal strength is the ability to bear and accept the existence of your limitations and failures while maintaining a friendly and open attitude towards yourself.

It's never too late to acknowledge a mistake. There may be something you need to make up for. Or maybe you just need to forgive yourself, confident that you did the best you could from what you knew at the time.

If you judge yourself harshly, you probably judge others harshly, too. If you are kind to yourself, you will naturally treat others the same way. And kindness can be catching; it can spread like ripples in water.

I hope this book has given you the ambition and the tools to work towards accepting yourself and the life you're living. And to look at yourself and others with kindness.

SUMMARY OF TOOLS

Below is a summary of the tools in this book. Not all of them are useful in every situation. Use the summary as an overview of all the possibilities and start with those that are most relevant to your situation.

Make up for a wrong

If you are genuinely sorry about something you've said or done, you can tell that to the person involved, perhaps even offer to make up for it. There's no statute of limitations on apologies. There's no reason why you can't return to a relationship several years later if there's something gnawing at you.

Read more about this in Chapter 2.

Revise your principles

Find out if the principles by which you live are appropriate to you and your situation. If it's too easy for you to feel guilty, your principles or rules of conduct are probably too strict.

Read more about this in Chapter 4.

Adjust your expectations for life

If you think you or your loved ones can get through life without failure, sorrow, and crisis, there will be far too much blame to share when the disappointments stream in and shock everyone.

Read more about this in Chapter 4.

Share blame with others

There's no reason to take all the blame yourself if it can be shared with others. Who else besides you has had an influence on a certain situation? Make a list and share the blame with all of them. If possible, attach a percentage of blame to each person. The more blame you give others, the less guilt you will feel. Even though you give some of the blame away, you can take full responsibility for getting the best out of the situation from now on. That's the wisest thing to do in some circumstances.

Read more about this in Chapter 3.

Direct some of your anger outward

Write letters to the others at fault, in which you confront them with their share of the blame and tell them what you believe they should do or have done. Don't send the letters; they are solely for your own sake. They might inspire you to speak to one or more of the other guilty parties in the situation you're in. Or maybe simply to look at yourself with kinder eyes.

Read more about this in Chapter 3.

Check to see if your guilty conscience is rational

Write a guilt letter and a letter of apology. While doing this, you will most likely discover an irrational part of your guilt that you can eliminate.

See the instructions in Chapter 11.

Forgive yourself

Make the decision to stop compensating for mistakes you've made. Don't punish yourself for the rest of your life. Focus instead on the opportunities you have from now on.

Read more about this in Chapter 10.

Check to see if other emotions are hidden

A guilty conscience sometimes covers up other emotions. Find out what you want or yearn for in a relationship.

Ask yourself:

- Is there something I feel bad about?
- Is there something I've lost?
- Is there something I miss?
- Am I angry at the person?
- Am I genuinely happy, even though I feel it's inappropriate?

Read more about this in Chapter 12.

Are you now, or have you ever been, in a relationship with someone lacking a sense of responsibility?

Make yourself aware of how relationships with people lacking responsibility can push you into being too responsible, which ends with you burdening yourself with guilt or responsibility that, in reality, belongs to others. You might need to put limits on your relationship with someone.

Read more about this in Chapter 9.

Abandon a fight by letting go

A guilty conscience is anger turned inward. Anger is the energy that comes from a fighting spirit. Sometimes the fight we are in can't be won, or perhaps it simply takes too much of a toll. Think about what you're fighting for and consider whether or not the goal is realistic. You might find a sense of relief by letting go of a hope and a fight.

Read more about this in Chapter 12.

Be friends with your guilty conscience

Often our biggest problem is everything we do to rid ourselves of it. Remind yourself that emotions aren't dangerous. They are welcome. Be curious about your guilt. Examine it. Don't let it lead you around by the nose. Be true to yourself and your values, and bear your guilt with dignity.

Read more about this in Chapter 5.

Think of your guilty conscience as an existential tax

When you do something other than what people close to you hope or expect, you might be afraid of their anger or judgment. Train yourself to be with your fear. And with your sorrow about not being able to make everyone happy. Tell yourself that your guilt is the price you pay for doing what genuinely feels right for yourself.

Read more about this in Chapter 5.

Give back responsibility

If sometime in the past you caused someone pain, you can express your remorse and regret about it. But don't continue doing so by compensating or thinking you're responsible for making sure the person has a good life. If that person is an adult, she's the only one truly able to bear that responsibility. You're doing her no favours by taking it on.

Read more about this in Chapter 11.

Acknowledge your guilt

If a decision you've made harms others, it's best for everyone if you acknowledge your guilt. Don't keep justifying your actions. It's brave and praiseworthy of you to bear your guilt. Feel how much you grow by doing so.

Read more about this in Chapter 10.

Speak kindly to yourself

Buy a notebook and use it to give yourself recognition for three concrete things every day for three or four months. This is how you train to see yourself with friendly eyes.

Read more about this in Chapter 2.

TEST

Do you easily develop a guilty conscience?

A guilty conscience has to do with relationships. In one relationship, you will immediately feel guilty about things you take much less seriously in another relationship. Therefore, you should think about one specific person when you take the test. If you take the test several times and each time think about a different person, you can compare your results.

Logically enough, this specific person you're examining in the test, the one involved in your bad conscience, I call *the person*. It can be your boyfriend, a friend, a parent, or a co-worker. In fact, it can be anyone you'd like to check your reactions to.

The results of the test will say something about you as well as the person and your relationship.

It's important that your answer is what first comes to mind; don't think too much about it. Don't read the conclusion of the test until after you've taken it because it might influence your results.

Put a number after every statement:

0 = Not true about me
1 = Slightly true about me
2 = Partly true about me
3 = Mostly true about me
4 = True about me

1. If the person and I plan on getting together, and I cancel on short notice, I get a guilty conscience.

_____

2. If I talk more than half the time when I'm with the person, I get a guilty conscience.

_____

3. If the person feels bad, I get a guilty conscience and feel that I should be doing more to help.

_____

4. If the person thinks I've ruined something for her, I feel bad and apologise.

_____

5. If the person visited me and the mood was a bit dreary, I wonder about what I did wrong.

_____

6. If I notice something about the person I don't like, I get a guilty conscience.

———

7. If I'm happy even though the person is feeling bad, I feel guilty.

———

8. If the person considers herself to be smarter, prettier, or better than I believe she is, I get a bad conscience about my less flattering opinion of her.

———

9. If the person gives me a disapproving look, I feverishly try to figure out what I can do to make her look at me with a happy expression.

———

10. If the person is feeling bad, I get a guilty conscience and rack my brain to find out what I've done wrong.

———

11. If the person is dissatisfied with something I do, I feel guilty and try to change my behaviour.

———

12. If I feel the urge to roll my eyes at something the person says, I get a guilty conscience.

____

13. If I feel the urge to say something true that would hurt the person, I get a guilty conscience.

____

14. If I feel so bad when I'm with the person that I don't have anything positive to contribute, I get a bad conscience.

____

15. If a conversation with the person is about something that doesn't interest me, I get a bad conscience if I don't take pains to listen closely.

____

16. If the person lets me know that she thinks highly of me, I get a guilty conscience if I don't feel the same way about her.

____

17. If the person invites me to her birthday party, and I'm not happy to get the invitation, I get a guilty conscience.

____

18. If the person proudly shows me something she has made, and I don't like it, I get a guilty conscience.

____

19. If I don't answer the phone when the person calls, I get a guilty conscience.

———

20. If I've forgotten the person's birthday, I get a guilty conscience.

———

21. If the person is sick, I get a guilty conscience for being well and happy.

———

22. If something I've said hurts the person, I get a guilty conscience, even though I didn't mean to hurt her.

———

23. If I'm more than fifteen minutes late when I'm meeting the person, I get a guilty conscience.

———

24. If I get annoyed at the person about something she can't do anything about, such as her appearance, I get a bad conscience.

———

Add the numbers up. The result will be between 0 and 96.

What a high score says about you

The higher your score, the more responsible you are, and the more likely you are to be burdened by a guilty conscience.

There are two types of statements in the test. The first group includes the numbers 6, 7, 8, 12, 13, 14, 16, 17, 18, 21, and 24. These statements measure your tendency towards irrational guilt. Write your numbers on the lines below and add them up.

6 ____

7 ____

8 ____

12 ____

13 ____

14 ____

16 ____

17 ____

18 ____

21 ____

24 ____

Total ____

Your score in Group 1 will be between 0 and 44.

Your Group 1 score

All the statements in Group 1 deal with things you have no control over. What you feel, for example, or what you want. In other words, an irrational guilty conscience and an exaggerated form of responsibility. Anything over 0 shows that you have experienced an irrational guilty conscience.

The closer your number is to 44, the better the following characteristics apply to you:

- You are someone people can count on.
- You feel strongly about wanting everyone around you to be happy all the time.
- You are an easy target for people wanting to unload their responsibility and guilt.
- It is so important for you to be a good friend/partner/parent that it borders on perfectionism.
- You take criticism hard because you tend to accept it without questioning whether there's the slightest bit of truth to it.
- It's difficult for you to set limits.
- You are an easy target for bullies.
- You are burdened by a guilty conscience and a feeling of inadequacy.

If you use the tools in this book to deal with your guilty conscience, your score in this group will fall, and your life will become easier.

Group 2

The statements in Group 2 measure a guilty conscience that might be rational. This group includes the numbers 1, 2, 3, 4, 5, 9, 10, 11, 15, 19, 20, 22, and 23. Write your numbers on the lines below and add them up.

1 _____

2 _____

3 _____

4 _____

5 _____

9 _____

10 _____

11 _____

15 _____

19 _____

20 _____

22 _____

23 _____

Total _____

Your score will be between 0 and 52.

Your score in Group 2

The closer your score is to 52, the more conscientious you are in your relationships. And the better the following characteristics apply to you:

- It's important to you to be a good friend and keep your word on what you agree to.
- If someone close by feels bad, you will do what you can to help.
- You are willing to consider if you're partly to blame for someone else's pain, and you're prepared to make amends for it if you are.
- If you've made a mistake, you don't need to be corrected by others because you'll immediately blame yourself and try to make sure it doesn't happen again.
- After a conflict, you are flexible and willing to meet halfway.
- It's important for you to be a decent person.

Even though all the statements in Group 2 deal with situations in which you have some influence, big or small, your feelings of guilt can be out of proportion. Your Group 2 score can therefore point to something about rational as well as irrational guilt.

Take the test with a few reservations

Remember that your result will differ depending on whom you're thinking of as you take the test. If the person is very close to you – your child, for example – your score will be higher than if you're less close to the person.

In addition, what a test can tell about a person is never comprehensive. There are far too many aspects that aren't included. Also, the result can vary depending on your situation or mood the day you take the test.

What a high score tells about the person or your relationship with the person

If you score higher in one of your relationships than in the others, it can say more about the relationship than about you. Consider if one or more of the statements below are true:

The person means a great deal to you

We have the strongest emotions for those we love the most. That goes for negative emotions, too, such as anger and guilt.

The person has a great deal of influence on your life or your situation

A boss, a landlady, a partner.

The person is dependent on you

If the person has a serious illness and she can't manage very well without your help, you naturally will assume more responsibility.

You mean a great deal to the person

You're aware that the person thinks very highly of you, and she will be more disappointed if you're the one who cancels a get-together, for example.

The person is your child, and she's a minor

We have a very special responsibility for our children when they are still young.

The person lacks a sense of responsibility

You notice perhaps that the person isn't doing well, but she's not taking responsibility for changing her situation or getting the necessary help. It's difficult for you to witness the person's pain.

The person sees herself as a better person

If the person sees herself as an innocent victim or superior to others, and perhaps even appears to be that way from the outside, you can easily end up with all the inadequacy. Some people have such a convincing manner and belief in their own perfection that the people around them tend to feel inadequate in some way.

The person has put you in a role you can't live up to

Perhaps one of your parents behaves irresponsibly, and they want you to take on the role of an adult and be responsible. Such an appeal can be nearly invisible to your consciousness. It can be a certain look, a facial expression, or a tone of voice that calls on you to take over. Another example of role confusion can arise if your partner acts as if you are her father or mother, and you feel pressured into loving her unconditionally, as parents ideally do. In that situation, you will probably experience a great deal of guilt at not being able to live up to that.

ACKNOWLEDGEMENTS

I wish to thank the following:

Registered psychotherapist and master of theology Bent Falk, who himself is the author of several books, including the bestseller *Honest Dialogue*. Bent Falk has been invaluable to me, both in my personal and professional development.

MSC in psychology and, until his death, head of the Institute for Gestalt Analysis Niels Hoffmeyer. He was a source of great inspiration to me for many years.

Thanks, too, to all of you who have read the book and given me feedback: Ellen Boelt, Margith Christiansen, Ene Esgaard, Christine Grøntved, Line Crump Horsted, Martin Håstrup, Kirstine Sand, and Knud Erik Andersen. Each of you has put your mark on this book.

LITERATURE

Buber, Martin: *I and Thou.* Martino Fine Books, 2010.

Davidsen-Nielsen, Marianne og Nini Leick: *Healing Pain: Attachment, Loss, and Grief Therapy.* Routledge, 1991.

Falk, Bent: *Honest Dialogue. Presence, common sense, and boundaries when you want to help someone.* Jessica Kingsley Publishers, 2017.

Hart, S. *Brain, Attachment, Personality: An Introduction to Neuroaffective Development.* London: Karnac Books 2018.

Jung, C. G.: *The Undiscovered Self.* Later Printing (6th) edition (1958)

Kierkegaard, Søren: *The Sickness unto Death.* Penguin Classics; First Printing edition (August 1, 1989)

Kierkegaard, Søren: *The Concept of Anxiety.* Princeton University Press; First Edition (US) First Printing edition (February 1, 1981)

Miller, Alice: *The Drama of the Gifted Child.* Basic Books, 1997

Della Selva, Patricia Coughlin: *Intensive Short-term Dynamic Psychotherapy: Theory and Technique.* London: Karnac Books. 1996.

O'toole, Donna: *Aarvy Aardvark Finds Hope.* Compassion Press, 1988.

Sand, Ilse: *Confronting Shame: How to Understand Your Shame and Gain Inner Freedom.* Jessica Kingsley Publishers, 2022

Sand, Ilse: *Highly Sensitive People in an Insensitive World: How to Create a Happy Life.* Jessica Kingsley Publishers, 2016.

Sand, Ilse: *On Being an Introvert or Highly Sensitive Person – a guide to boundaries, joy, and meaning.* Jessica Kingsley Publishers, 2018

Sand, Ilse: *The Emotional Compass: How to Think Better about Your Feelings.* Jessica Kingsley Publishers, 2016.

Sand, Ilse: *Helping Through Conversation. Specific advice, ideas and instructions.* Ammentorp 2023

Yalom, Irvin D: *Existential Psychotherapy,* 1980.

BY THE SAME AUTHOR

Confronting Shame: How to Understand Your Shame and Gain Inner Freedom

A book about letting go of the fear that something is wrong with you. How you can understand your shame and the problems it causes.

Come Closer: On Love and Self-Protection

On how unconscious self-protection strategies can get in the way of vibrant, loving connections and how these strategies can be fought by making them conscious.

Do You Miss Someone? How to heal a damaged relationship – or let it go

Various strategies can help if you want to re-establish or improve — or perhaps end — a relationship.

The Emotional Compass: How to Think Better about Your Feelings

On what feelings can mean and how to get in touch with them.

Highly Sensitive People in an Insensitive World: How to Create a Happy Life

On highly sensitive people and shame, guilt, and communication.

Helping Through Conversation: Specific advice, ideas and instructions

On how to use psychotherapeutic tools in supportive dialogues – and how to take care of yourself as a helper.

On Being an Introvert or Highly Sensitive Person – *a guide to boundaries, joy, and meaning*

What does it mean to be an introvert or highly sensitive?

And what is the difference?

Good advice and tools for handling different situations with which introverts and highly sensitive people often have difficulty.

Read more at ilsesand.com.